Seduced by Story

Also by Peter Brooks

Balzac's Lives

Seduced by Story

The Use and Abuse of Narrative

PETER BROOKS

 **New York Review Books** New York

This is a New York Review Book
published by The New York Review of Books
207 East 32nd Street, New York, NY 10016
www.nyrb.com

Library of Congress Cataloging-in-Publication Data
Names: Brooks, Peter, 1938– author.
Title: Seduced by story / by Peter Brooks.
Description: New York : New York Review Books, 2022 .
Identifiers: LCCN 2021050594 | ISBN 9781681376639 (paperback) | ISBN
    9781681376646 (ebook)
Subjects: LCSH: Narration (Rhetoric) | Storytelling—Philosophy.
Classification: LCC PN212 .B766 2022 | DDC 808/.036—dc23eng/20211103
LC record available at https://lccn.loc.gov/2021050594

ISBN 978-1-68137-663-9
Available as an electronic book; ISBN 978-1-68137-664-6

Printed in the United States of America on acid-free paper.

10 9 8 7 6 5 4 3 2

Contents

Foreword

BACK IN 1984, I published a book called *Reading for the Plot*, which recorded my discovery of the crucial importance of narrative, of storytelling, and how we can understand it. The opening sentences of that book:

> Our lives are ceaselessly intertwined with narrative, with the stories that we tell and hear told, those we dream or imagine or would like to tell, all of which are reworked in that story of our own lives that we narrate to ourselves in an episodic, sometimes semiconscious, but virtually uninterrupted monologue. We live immersed in narrative, recounting and reassessing the meaning of our past actions, anticipating the outcome of our future projects, situating ourselves at the intersection of several stories not yet completed.

I still believe that, but here I want to record my somewhat disabused sense of what has happened to "narrative" in our culture in the decades since that book. It's a curious story.

1. Stories Abounding

The World Overtaken by Narrative

"There's nothing in the world more powerful than a good story. Nothing can stop it. No enemy can defeat it." Thus spake Tyrion in the final episode of the television series *Game of Thrones*, claiming the throne for Bran the Broken. Many viewers liked neither the choice of king nor its rationale. But the claim that story brings you to world dominance seems by now so banal that it's common wisdom. Narrative seems to have become accepted as the only form of knowledge and speech that regulates human affairs.

For myself, the moment I knew narrative had taken over the world came with President George W. Bush's presentation of his cabinet, in December 2000. Said Bush of his appointees: "Each person has got their own story that is so unique, stories that really explain what America can and should be about." And more simply, in presenting Secretary of State Colin Powell: "a great American story." And simpler still, in introducing Secretary of Transportation Norman Y. Mineta: "I love his story." One had the impression that Bush's understanding of reality was wholly narrative. No other form of speech or cognitive faculty came close.

Bush gave dramatic confirmation to the notion that narrative is the crucial tool in the toolkit we use to construct our knowledge of the world and our sense of self. This left me pensive, and not a little confused. It was as if a fledgling I had nourished had become a predator devouring reality in the name of story. Since the early 1970s, I had been arguing and teaching that narrative is in fact key to our understanding of self and surround: that we live in and by what the psychologist Jerome Bruner later labeled the narrative construction of reality.[1] This was not at all common wisdom at the time, but rather a kind of anthropological take on narrative largely inspired by French structural linguists, anthropologists, and literary theorists. With a few colleagues I taught a course on "Fictions and the Forms of Narrative" that asked questions not only about the formal structures of stories but also about their purpose and project; and not only literary narratives but stories told in advertising and myth and dreams. We saw narrative as one of the large categories by which we try to understand the world and construct its meanings. We were seconded in this effort by what would soon be called the "narrative turn" in psychology and philosophy, and eventually in medicine and economics. Gradually we learned that we were part of a larger movement to understand the uses of the narratives that surround us, from the everyday to the transcendent.[2] But we never envisaged nor hoped for the kind of narrative takeover of reality we appear to be witnessing in the early twenty-first century, where even public civic discourse supposedly dedicated to reasoned analysis seems to have been taken hostage. This narrative takeover—what it means, how to think about it, and how to provide a more intelligent account of what narrative is and does—motivates me here.

"Numberless are the world's narratives." So began Roland Barthes in his "Introduction to the Structural Analysis of Narrative," published in 1966—an essay that was the inaugural gesture for the new discipline of narratology, the methodical analysis of narrative.[3] "There isn't, there has never been anywhere, any people without narrative," wrote Barthes. "International, transhistorical, transcultural, narrative is there, like life." Stories (unlike poems) can be translated, they can be transposed to other media, they can be summarized, they can be retold "in other words" and yet still be recognizably the same story. Narrative, which the human child appears to discover before age three, is fundamental to our sense of reality and how it is ordered. We don't simply arrange random facts into narratives; our sense of the way stories go together, how life is made meaningful as narrative, presides at our choice of facts as well, and the ways we present them. Our daily lives, our daydreams, our sense of self are all constructed as stories.

What seems obvious often can open the richest insight once we look at it closely. That surely has been the case with narrative: once under-studied, it is now the object of fine analytic discrimination. Meanwhile, the plethoric spread of narrative in public life has gone forward, taking no apparent account of the analysts, though one senses that the two developments cannot be unrelated in some large cultural sense. The French philosopher Jean-François Lyotard claimed that in our postmodernist moment the "grand narratives" that sustained whole societies, the narrative of emancipation especially, have lost their force.[4] We are left with many mini-narratives everywhere, individual or collective and, in many cases, dominantly narcissistic and self-serving. I look at the package containing the cookies I just bought and find it wants to tell me "Our Story." I go to order furniture online and I encounter a tab labeled, again, "Our

Story": "Steve Conine and Niraj Shah met as high school students attending a summer program at Cornell University. They both went on to study engineering at Cornell and quickly struck up a friendship while they were freshmen living in the same dorm. During their final semester of college, Steve and Niraj both enrolled in a class on entrepreneurism which sparked a business plan that turned into their first company and, ultimately, became the foundation for founding and building several businesses in the technology sector." (Not clear why *this* story is supposed to foster confidence in the purchaser.) At Tom's of Maine, it's called "The Backstory": "Tom and Kate Chappell moved to Maine from Philadelphia in 1968, looking for a healthier, simpler life for their growing family. They discovered the benefits of natural and unprocessed food, and started looking for the same qualities in personal care products. But all they found were labels listing artificial flavors, fragrances, sweeteners, colors and preservatives. So they decided to create their own." J. Crew offers "Our Story" as well. Also Procter & Gamble. Johnson & Johnson has an elaborate and illustrated "Our Stories" in several chapters. Snapchat in 2015 introduced a feature called "Our Story" that aggregates individuals participating in a particular event. A 2020 *New York Times* news story questioning the accuracy of one of its own reporters, Rukmini Callimachi, noted a "profound shift" underway at the *Times*: "The paper is in the midst of an evolution from the stodgy paper of record into a juicy collection of great narratives, on the web and streaming services."[5] Readers of the *Times* have noticed that nearly every article now begins, often tediously, with an anecdote leading in to the substance of the subject.

Some more examples: according to French sociologist Christian Salmon, it was former journalist David Gergen as adviser to President Ronald Reagan who created the crucial notion of the "story of the day," which would be presented ready-made to the media to feed on, comment on, disseminate.[6] That continues, in more and more virulent form, as rulers judge that controlling the media narrative is what governing is all about. "The nation needs a better story about the drivers of economic growth," I read in *The New York Times*.[7] Writing to the corporate world in *Whoever Tells the Best Story Wins*, Annette Simmons claims: "The really important issues of this world are ultimately decided by the story that grabs the most attention and is repeated most often."[8] That seems truer with every passing day, as Twitter and the meme dominate the presentation of reality. Simmons goes on to maintain that "every problem in the world can be addressed—solved, made bearable, even eliminated—with better storytelling." Her book "should give you tools to make more money, increase cooperation, and decrease resistance in any situation." National Public Radio's StoryCorps project presents a more communitarian but no less laudatory view of storytelling: "StoryCorps' mission is to preserve and share humanity's stories in order to build connections between people and create a more just and compassionate world. We do this to remind one another of our shared humanity, to strengthen and build the connections between people, to teach the value of listening, and to weave into the fabric of our culture the understanding that everyone's story matters. At the same time, we are creating an invaluable archive for future generations."[9] Seth Godin, who runs the Story Skills Workshop, much appreciated in the corporate world, posted his response to the events roiling the United States in the summer of 2020: "The way forward is through. Through empathy and through practice. We are each charged with standing up and telling our story, a true story of possibility, as we weave together a better future. We've all seen, firsthand, the effect of a powerful story. This proven workshop will help you craft one that makes things better."[10] The story of a "stolen election" led to the violent invasion of the U.S. Capitol a few months later.

One could continue to pile up examples. Every person has a story to tell, and the corporate person has understood, with a vengeance, that it must stake its identity, persuasion, and profits on telling a story, however bizarre or banal. Corporate reports have turned from the statistical to the narrative mode. And in the wake of the corporation are political candidates and parties, the military, the tourism industry, universities, hospitals, bakeries—even accounting firms. Salmon, the sociologist, has identified what he calls a "*nouvel ordre narratif*," or NON: a new narrative order that dominates in business and politics. He notes that such a corporation as Enron, which famously went bust in 2001, seems to have been built uniquely on stories—fictions, in fact—that had little to do with the company's balance sheet but rather with a kind of imaginary accounting that generated stories of impending great wealth. According to Salmon, the new attention to narrative in philosophy and ethics and literary theory and history writing came to affect corporate management, and then the military, which needed positive narratives to undergird the dubious wars it was made to wage. Ronald Reagan, ever telling anecdotes—minimal stories—appeared to govern largely by story, at times confounding the real with films in which he had played a role.[11] Since Reagan, storytelling has become so ubiquitous that it's hard to know where to begin in a discussion of its nature, its parts, its spread, and its power. A stark example: the Starr Report prepared for the impeachment of President Clinton in the matter of Monica Lewinsky chose to present its major findings in a section titled simply: "The Narrative." A kind of preemptive strike, as if to say: this is the way it happened; there is no other version.

This mindless valorization of storytelling speaks to crucial facts in contemporary culture that need more analysis. Why is it that other forms of presentation and understanding have been largely abandoned in favor of telling stories? I recall, from an age still dominated by radio, the singing commercial, so memorable that a number of them still come to mind:

> I'm Chiquita Banana and I've come to say
> Bananas have to ripen in a certain way—
> And when they're flecked with brown and have a golden hue
> Bananas taste the best and are the best for you...

That lyric debuted in 1944. Or the Ballantine beer poems:

> In Fourteen Hundred and Ninety-two
> Columbus sailed the ocean blue,
> The trip was hot—
> His crew kept cryin'
> "Ask the man for Ballantine."

Or as we entered the television age, the commercial that simply foregrounded a product with a crooning lyric to accompany it, as for Miller beer:

> When it's time to relax, Miller stands clear.
> Beer after beer.
> One thing stands clear

If you've got the time
We've got the beer. Miller beer.

Why has the lyric, a compact and emotionally charged form of communication, been completely eclipsed by the more discursive and additive form that is narrative?

The results of what I see as the storification of reality may be simplistic, but I don't think the causes are simple. Could it be that the current hyperinflation of story is linked, however distantly, to the new critical attention to narrative and its analysis that began in the 1960s? An unintended consequence of some magnitude, but possibly the case. Our present world of pervasive storying was underwritten and, I believe, preceded by a well-recognized narrative turn in several serious fields of thought. History, which some decades back seemed to have set aside storytelling in favor of demographic and social analyses of selected moments and places, appears to have returned to full-throated storytelling. Philosophy, especially moral philosophy (though perhaps still dominated by logical and linguistic analysis), also found strong advocates for narrative, such as Paul Ricoeur, Richard Rorty, Alasdair MacIntyre, and Charles Taylor. They make implicit or explicit claims that human institutions and behaviors can be grasped only through stories. In economics, too, which might seem exempt from narrative thinking, the likes of D. N. McCloskey and the Nobel-winning Robert Shiller have argued for narrative as part of the discipline. In psychology, Jerome Bruner in particular stressed that young children initially learn not through "scientific" experimentation on reality but through swapping stories about it. Rita Charon and her followers have insisted on the importance of "narrative medicine," based on listening to patients' stories and reciprocating with stories about illness and recovery—and death. Narrative as explanation once seemed to belong to an older paradigm—one elaborated largely in the nineteenth century, the golden age of historical and evolutionary thought—but now it is back, as if to emphasize that the time-boundedness of human life is the crucial human problem. Mortality can perhaps best be dealt with in story form. Whatever meanings life may have, or fail to have, develop through time. As the finale of Lin-Manuel Miranda's *Hamilton* asks, with a poignancy to which any of us can respond: "Who lives, who dies, who tells your story?"

Narrative plays a *constitutive* role in a number of the disciplines in which we seek and impart knowledge. One of the most thoughtful analysts of historical writing, Louis O. Mink, has reflected on the uses of narrative in making sense of historical events, neither rejecting narrative history (as certain quantitative historians claimed to do) nor investing narrative with truth-value on its own. He makes the point that the past comes into existence only insofar as we tell stories about it. "There can in fact be no untold stories at all, just as there can be no unknown knowledge. There can only be past facts not yet described in a context of narrative form."[12] If this claim may pass muster in the writing of history, it takes on a more radical edge when it is used to describe how the law works. Anthony Amsterdam and Jerome Bruner state in *Minding the Law* that the traditional view that adjudication could proceed by "examining free-standing factual data selected on grounds of their logical pertinency" has been superseded by the view that "increasingly we are coming to recognize that both the questions and the answers in such matters of 'fact' depend largely upon one's choice (considered or unconsidered) of some overall narrative as best describing *what happened* or *how the world works.*"[13] In other words, the "facts on the ground" are not cognizable at all until we make them into a narrative, and that narrative and its meaning are not determined by the facts but shaped by our expectations of narrative coherence and meaning, which in turn can derive from our preformed beliefs about human behavior, motivation, morality, gender identity, and so on.

Legal adjudication doesn't in theory make a place for storytelling, though narrative may be crucial in creating facts, judgments, verdicts. Stories are regarded by law as suspiciously emotional, as making a kind of appeal to empathy—or prejudice—that legal rules must cabin and confine.[14] Yet there is ample evidence that the law relies far more than it is aware on stories, not only those of the courtroom —usually opposing stories, one of which will trump the other—but also at the appellate level, where the "facts of the case" established at trial must be retold as part of the attempt to judge whether the case has been decided according to the legal rules. And there are other stories as well: those of precedential cases, and maybe of the Constitution—its text and how it was decided upon and interpreted. The uses of story in the law and the law's seeming blindness to its storied nature need pondering: I've added to the first five chapters of this book a sixth specifically on the question of law's stories.

Bruner offers what may be the baseline claim for the importance of narrative in his essay "The Narrative Construction of Reality." He argues that too much work in cognitive psychology has studied young children as if they were baby scientists, discovering how the world works and how to live their lives by testing reality. For Bruner, the budding scientist model is misleading. Children learn far more through their narrative interactions with parents, caregivers, siblings, playmates. They tell one another stories about how things work and about what behaviors mean, including the arcane world of adult behavior. Children develop theories in story form about all sorts of things, very much including the world of adult sexuality, as Freud maintained, and as Charlotte Brontë and Henry James and Marcel Proust in their various ways dramatized. And of course myths are usually stories about something that cannot be explained through logical reasoning—origins, for instance, or the meaning of death. Story may be a necessary part of our cognitive interaction with the world because its mode of explaining takes place within time, and humans are time-bound in a way that they are not place-bound. Story is the *logic* of explanations and meanings that unfold in time, the logic of those who are mortal. When at the end of his long journey Proust's hero discovers his vocation, he is called to write a book that will have the "shape of time."

It is not always clear whether thinkers associated with the narrative turn want to make an ontological or an epistemological claim for narrative: whether they see narrative as constitutive of human existence, and humans defined as *Homo narrans*, or rather conceive narrative as the mental instrument that humans use to make sense of an otherwise unorganized existence.[15] I am not sure that we are in a position to answer that question. If, as Bruner suggests, our earliest negotiations with others and with our surroundings come in story form, it is difficult to say whether that means we are hard-wired narrativists or rather that our earliest mental training takes narrative form.

What seems more important than choosing between ontology and epistemology is recognizing that telling and living are not the same thing. We may live the world as an unfurling narrative, but when we tell of it, whether anecdotally or analytically, that's a different operation. Confusions arise, not least in legal adjudication, when there is no distinction made between what happened and the telling of what happened—even if it is often the case that we can know what happened only through versions of its telling. The universe is not our stories about the universe, even if those stories are all we have. Swamped in story as we seem to be, we may lose the distinction between the two, asserting the dominion of our constructed realities over the real thing.

The proliferation of storytelling throughout social institutions of all types may have trivialized the notion of narrative, but narrative isn't itself a trivial phenomenon. It responds, however obtusely or exploitatively, to a new awareness that reality as we experience it is to a large degree narratively constructed. It's of course not narrative construction that is new: on the contrary, the work of a mythographer such as Claude Lévi-Strauss suggests that understanding reality through narrative belongs to all peoples everywhere. Epic storytelling, for instance, undergirds cultural identity in many parts of the world. What's new is an increased recognition of the permeating cultural importance of narrative. You find the essence of that recognition within Western culture as early as Aristotle's *Poetics*, with its assertion of the primacy of *mythos*, story or plot, in the construction of tragedy. But I'd trace our current preoccupation with story to twentieth-century attempts to understand the construction of stories, beginning with those labeled Russian Formalists, a remarkable group who flourished after the Revolution until Stalin put an end to them. They were attentive precisely to the constructedness of literary artifacts. The title of Boris Eikhenbaum's essay "How Gogol's *Overcoat* Was Made" sets the tone. Characteristic too is Vladimir Propp's *Morphology of the Folktale* (1928), in which he selects one hundred Russian tales classified by collectors of folklore as "fairy tales" and analyzes them in terms of functions and agents, showing how most tales follow a similar sequence of functions ("an act of character, defined from the point of view of its significance for the course of the action") and use a generic cast of characters, whatever names they may be given. Function and sequence become for Propp powerful tools of analysis. And for the Russian Formalists as a group, this type of operation—identifying functional units and how they combine—brought to the fore the importance of identifying the building materials of fictional construction.[16] The group was part of a large modern movement to formalize our knowledge of cultural artifacts.

I don't think it is pedantic to urge that a fundamental distinction advanced by the Russian Formalists remains crucial to any serious discussion of narrative: the distinction between *fabula* and *sjuzhet*. Fabula is the story told, the events recounted, in their "natural" chronological order, whereas sjuzhet is the presentation of events in the narrative we read or listen to—events that may not fall in chronological order, that may be, will almost certainly be, rearranged, shaded, enlarged, minimized, distorted. Events are ordered, usually with some design and intention. Thus sjuzhet is not innocent: it is a take on a story, a perspective, an arrangement. Yet a moment's reflection shows us that most often we know the fabula, what happened, only by way of the sjuzhet. The distinction between story and its telling has immediate consequences in many domains—in the law, for instance, where "just the facts" always must be recounted, given narrative form, with crucial consequences for the outcome.

The enterprise of the Russian Formalists found new life in French Structuralist "narratology," especially in work by Barthes, Tzvetan Todorov, and Gérard Genette. There may be no direct link between these analysts of story and the captivation of corporate and political worlds by storytelling, though the spread of an interest in narrative and its analysis to the American university in the 1970s and '80s no doubt had something to do with the new cultural valorization of story and its power. What Barthes dubbed "narrativity"—all those signals that we have entered a story world—clearly became crucial in culture.[17] We live much of our lives well within the orbit of narrativity. The historian Carlo Ginzburg claims that modern "sciences of man" often operate with an "evidential paradigm" that involves knowing by way of clues, following the traces left by one's quarry. This is a science of the concrete and particular that achieves its discoveries through putting particulars together in a narrative chain. Ginzburg identifies it with the huntsman's lore:

> Man has been a hunter for thousands of years. In the course of countless pursuits he learned to reconstruct the shapes and movements of his invisible prey from tracks in the mud, broken branches, droppings of excrement, tufts of hair, entangled feathers, stagnating odors. He learned to sniff out, record, interpret, and classify such infinitesimal traces as trails of spittle. He learned how to execute complex mental operations with lightning speed, in the depth of a forest or in a prairie with its hidden dangers.[18]

Even in a post-hunting society, searches achieve their discoveries by such tracking of details, making them into a chain of meaning, uncovering their connections. Ginzburg speculates that this kind of knowing may in fact lie at the inception of narrative itself: the data gathered by the huntsman must be "arranged by the observer in such a way as to produce a narrative sequence, which could be expressed most simply as 'someone passed this way.'" Narrative may be a cognitive instrument of a specific type, one "invented" for the decipherment of details of the real that take on their meaning only when linked in a series, enchained in a manner that allows one to detect that "someone passed this way." This is what Sherlock Holmes's searches are all about—picking out those details of reality that prove meaningful as clues. And the huntsman's paradigm may indicate in more general terms the use-value of narrative as a form of speech and cognition: it is the instrument we use when the putting together of particulars into a meaningful sequence seems to be the only way to track down our quarry, whatever it may be.

Behind Ginzburg's suggestive hypotheses lies the nineteenth century's discovery that certain kinds of explanation—in geology, philology, and evolutionary biology, for example—necessarily work through narrative. Charles Darwin's narratives of evolutionary change are crucial to much modern explanation.[19] Psychoanalysis, for instance, and also the "case method" of legal reasoning, depend crucially on a narrative account, reasoning from present phenomena, such as a patient's symptoms or a dispute about the applicability of a legal doctrine, back along a narrative path in search of causes and origins that then, plotted forward, explain how the present came to be as it is. In even broader terms, we might say that narrative becomes a necessary form of knowing with the emergence, in the Enlightenment, from a culture dominated by a sacred explanation of the human condition into a new secular world where humans are on their own and must explain themselves to themselves.

Narrative in this view is indispensable, though not universally so. The evidential paradigm does not give legitimacy to the unthinking proliferation of narrative that we encounter in contemporary culture. We may be able to specify the kinds of problems that narrative alone can illuminate, and others where we prefer to think in different kinds of discourse. Consider that the structural linguist Roman Jakobson distinguished two poles of language, each associated with a type of aphasia.[20] At one pole the speaker cannot combine words into a significant sequence; at the other, the speaker cannot select the appropriate word. The former shows a breakdown in the axis of combination, the metonymic function; the latter a breakdown in the axis of selection, the metaphoric function. In Jakobson's interpretation (which modifies the use of these terms in classical rhetoric), metaphor, the axis of selection, is typified by lyric poetry—its emphasis on the palpability of language, its structuring by rhyme and parallelism and echo. Metonymy comes to the fore in narrative, particularly in the nineteenth-century realist tradition, where we work from one detail to another, achieving wholeness only through the linkage and accumulation of detail.

On this theory, narrative is one of the large categories in our use of language to represent the world—but not the only one. The distinction may put us on notice that the neglect of one pole for the other ought to arouse our critical attention: something has been skewed. The seeming obliteration in the public sphere of other forms of expression by narrative suggests that something in our culture has gone astray. Do we really want all our understandings to be expressed in narrative terms? Isn't there a risk of making "story" an excuse from other kinds of understanding? What about logical argument, for instance, once considered the dominant form of civic discourse? If

I tell my story—if a corporation tells its story—does that absolve either of the need to explain myself or itself? One has the impression that storytelling can sometimes be an evasion. By claiming a kind of exemplary status by way of one's story you excuse yourself from other forms of justification. Recall the claim of Annette Simmons: "Every problem in the world can be addressed—solved, made bearable, even eliminated—with better storytelling." Do we really want to subscribe to that belief? Doesn't it mystify more than it solves?

A persuasive critique of the dominant narrative paradigm has been voiced by the philosopher Galen Strawson. He protests especially against the notion that "the self" must be narrative:

> "Self is a perpetually rewritten story," according to the psychologist Jerome Bruner; we are all constantly engaged in "self-making narrative" and "in the end we *become* the autobiographical narratives by which we 'tell about' our lives." Oliver Sacks agrees: each of us "constructs and lives a 'narrative'. . . this narrative *is* us, our identities." A vast chorus of assent arises from the humanities—literary studies, psychology, anthropology, sociology, philosophy, political theory, religious studies, echoed back by psychotherapy, medicine, law, marketing, design: human beings typically experience their lives as a narrative or story of some sort, or at least as a collection of stories.[21]

This constitutes what Strawson calls the "psychological Narrativity thesis," which he finds falsifies his own experience as well as that of others who feel no need to see their lives in narrative terms. They do not subscribe to the idea of a "Storied Self," to cite the title of another of Strawson's essays. Strawson often finds the psychological thesis coupled to the "ethical Narrativity thesis," which states that constructing the narrative of one's own life is somehow vital to richly aware personhood. Strawson cites a number of philosophers who appear to hold that view: Charles Taylor, who writes that a "basic condition of making sense of ourselves [is] that we grasp our lives in a *narrative*," that we understand our lives "as an unfolding story."[22] And Alasdair MacIntyre: "The unity of a human life is the unity of a narrative quest."[23] And so on. The proliferation of memoir and "autofiction" in our culture fits the same claim.

The issues raised here are tricky. Strawson claims: "Your 'narrative' is something you can try to work out, should you wish to, looking back; but you shouldn't expect to get it right, or let it dictate your stance to the future." I agree, but it doesn't seem to me so simple. I do believe we try to understand what our lives have meant, if anything, and to do so we have to order our lives in narrative form: that is the shape we give to whatever unfolds in time. It's quite true that we can't ever find the proper repose, as Kierkegaard puts it, to see our lives in full retrospect. That view is denied to us. According to Walter Benjamin, this explains why we read fiction: we seek in the death of the fictional character the meaning of life that comes only with death. Death in fiction is the "flame" at which we warm "our shivering lives."[24]

Consider that our conception of "self" in contemporary culture owes much to psychoanalytic thinking, and that Freud's understanding of self is resolutely narrative, though not in any simple sense. The narrative of the past worked out in psychotherapy may be a blend of fact and fiction: its test lies more in its therapeutic results than in its verifiability.[25] The analysand needs to reach a coherent story of who he or she is. But developing a narrative is a tool toward self-understanding rather than the goal. Strawson's critique of the position that equates the self with the narrative told about it carries weight. He agrees with what appears to be Jean-Paul Sartre's argument, in his novel *Nausea* (*La Nausée*), that "self-storying, although inevitable, condemns us to inauthenticity, a kind of absence from our own lives."[26] But does Strawson understand the force of his concessive—"although inevitable"—here? Telling the story of oneself to oneself does seem absolutely inevitable if one is not to live life unthinkingly. We assess ourselves in terms of the story up till now, and we project future chapters. That conceiving our lives in narrative form can falsify experience and lead us astray rather than to the truth seems true enough, but that doesn't mean we can live without telling.

It might seem that I should share Strawson's positions given my own unease with the proliferation of narrative and inflated claims about its capacity to solve all personal and social issues. I am sympathetic to his critique of extreme narrativism, especially the implicit claim that living is identical to one's telling about living. But rather than invalidating the narrativist position in general Strawson, in my view, points to the necessity and inevitability of narrative in the construction of our lives and our understandings of reality. If narrative can't be the sole tool—as Jakobson's two poles of language suggest—it also can't be dismissed. Strawson's rejection of narrative may be usefully polemical but it cannot be our resting place. What we need may rather be an analytic unpacking of the claims for narrative, a clearer understanding of what it can and cannot accomplish. A more ambitious set of analytic tools for studying how narrative works may be required to get beyond Strawson's oppositions.

To move toward a conclusion to this first foray into our subject, let me mention a famous story by Jorge Luis Borges, "Tlön, Uqbar, Orbis Tertius," which describes the creation of an imaginary world from the "conjunction of a mirror and an encyclopedia": a world that reflects the real world but in a context of extreme idealism, one where realism is considered exotic, and refutable. Borges's postface to this tale published in 1940 is dated, proleptically, 1947, and it describes with great prescience how the rise of fascism would destroy realism, substituting for reality an ideology that dictates a totalistic new interpretation of the world.

> Almost immediately, reality yielded on more than one account. The truth is that it longed to yield. Ten years ago any symmetry with a resemblance of order—dialectical materialism, anti-Semitism, Nazism—was sufficient to entrance the minds of men. How could one do other than submit to Tlön, to the minute and vast evidence of an orderly planet? It is useless to answer that reality is also orderly. Perhaps it is, but in accordance with divine laws—I translate: inhuman laws—which we never quite grasp. Tlön is surely a labyrinth, but it is a labyrinth devised by men, a labyrinth destined to be deciphered by men.
>
> The contact and the habit of Tlön have disintegrated this world. Enchanted by its rigor, humanity forgets over and again that it is a rigor of chess masters, not of angels.[27]

What Borges describes, I believe, is what happens when stories become myths: when their status as fictions, *ficciones*, is forgotten and they are taken as real explanations of the world, as something other than "as if" constructions, as the object of belief.[28] On the basis of such fictions become myths we erect theologies. Very much including political theologies. But even without that fearful and all too present outcome, we may find ourselves inertly accepting the notion that all is story, and that the best story wins. Borges, himself a master storyteller, puts us on warning that we must remain critical of the all-encompassing claims of story. We need to oppose critical and analytical intelligence to narratives that seduce us into the acceptance of dominant ideologies. We need as listeners and readers to resist a passive narcosis of response.

Borges's story may also remind us of the conflicts over the representation of history that have riven the American public in our time. How history is written, taught, visually represented has come to be a battleground. The plan to exhibit the *Enola Gay*—the plane that delivered the atomic bomb that destroyed Hiroshima—at the Smithsonian Institution set off a classic confrontation about how history should be told.[29] More recently, the enduring legacy of American slavery and its aftermaths has been once again brought to the forefront of public consciousness, in disputes over history textbooks and public monuments. The *New York Times* journalist Ezra Klein summed up the situation: "You've heard plenty by now about the fight over teaching critical race theory and the 1619 Project. But behind these skirmishes is something deeper: A fight over the story we tell about America."[30] Very true: something more must be at stake for a recondite academic discourse, critical race theory, and a journalistic series on the place of slavery in American history to become politically controversial and divisive. The *Times*'s description of the 1619 Project—named for the year slaves first were brought to Virginia—suggests the deep divide:

> The goal of The 1619 Project is to reframe American history by
> considering what it would mean to regard 1619 as our nation's birth
> year. Doing so requires us to place the consequences of slavery and
> the contributions of black Americans at the very center of the story
> we tell ourselves about who we are as a country.[31]

A kind of history subversive of the usual tale, told from the other
side of the divide.

I experienced the different public stories spun from disputed
histories soon after I went to teach at the University of Virginia,
twenty-some years ago. I went to a law office in downtown Charlottesville to sign a document: I was shocked by the massive eques-
trian statues of Generals Robert E. Lee and Stonewall Jackson, and
by another statue of Johnny Reb, that dominated Court Square and
Market Square parks. As a lifelong Northerner, I was ambivalent
about my move to "the South" in the first place, and these commem-
orations of the leaders of rebellion made me feel I was on alien
ground, and unwelcome there. I could only imagine what African
Americans thought of such dominant tributes to the defense of their
enslavement. These statues, like so many others across the states of
the former Confederacy, had been erected in the early twentieth
century (1917 and 1919), when the history of the "lost cause" had
been fully rewritten in *Gone with the Wind* mode: a gallant struggle
of the aristocratic, agrarian South to preserve its "values" against
the crass Northern oppressor. The statues emerged suddenly into
national notoriety in the summer of 2017: the city's decision to
remove them was countered by the "Unite the Right" rally, which
brought a collection of white supremacist and other such groups to
Charlottesville in what became a deadly riot: an event that emblem-

atized the Trump era's deference to those who rose in opposition to contemporary demands for equality, including a new accountability for the history of slavery.

On July 10, 2021, some three months after the Virginia Supreme Court overturned a lower court ruling that they must remain in place, the statues of Lee and Jackson were hoisted from their pedestals and loaded onto flatbed trucks, to be warehoused until a suitable context for their display could be found—presumably in a museum that would explain how they came to be, rather than a site of public celebration. Meanwhile, in 2020 the University of Virginia completed a memorial to the four thousand enslaved laborers who built Thomas Jefferson's "academical village," a circular granite monument sunk in the earth some distance from the Rotunda that dominates the university. The memorial, which clearly owes something to Maya Lin's Vietnam Veterans Memorial, represents not only in its subject but in its form a quiet riposte to the heroic mounted statues of Confederate generals that once dominated many southern towns but may now be largely headed to the dustbins of history. Statues and monuments are historical narratives frozen into striking visual and tactile moments—in Jakobson's terms, metonyms become metaphors: attempts to seize and finalize historical meanings in stone and bronze. Their placement and history, the calls for and protests against their removal, then proposals for counter-monuments in commemoration of the oppressed and forgotten of history: experiencing the life of public historical commemorative art today bears conclusive testimony that, as William Faulkner put it, the past is not dead; it isn't even past. History lives and changes shape in our reinterpretations of it. This is true of course not only for the United States: witness, for instance, how France has slowly come to terms with its history of collaboration with the Nazi occupier, and the role of writers and filmmakers in the revision of the image of this past. Or Britain's gradually evolving revision of its imperial past and its icons, including such individuals as Cecil Rhodes. The American experience is particularly fraught because of the fact of enslavement, as well as the near genocide of its indigenous peoples. The continuing battle over the meanings of American history plays out in a very visible public sphere, in what you might call monument speak. It is further testimony that controlling the narrative, in this case the narrative of who we may be as a people and a nation, is of vital importance. The battle over representations of history makes manifest how crucial the stories we tell can be in our claims to identity and to self-knowledge.

How to sort this all out? Can it be sorted out? A pervasive narrativism dominates in our culture. We need to ask further why this is so, why other forms of exposition and self-presentation seem to have been thoroughly eclipsed by story. But we can't begin to critique the misuses, and mindless uses, of narrative without further analysis. I believe that the only way to address the overabundance of story is through the analytic study of story, by way of what the French Structuralists dubbed "narratology." I don't by any means intend to deploy all the technicity of narratology, which has become an analytic discipline of greater refinement than most of us need or want. But attention to the ways that narrative works as system and as rhetoric—that is, as means of persuasion—should prove useful in promoting clarity of thought about our desire and our need for narrative. In what follows I try to view with a critical eye the implications of the narrative turn in different kinds of storytelling, across different fields of knowledge.

2. The Epistemology of Narrative; or, How Can the Teller Know the Tale?

"EPISTEMOLOGY" SOUNDS PRETENTIOUS. But what I mean is simple: How do those who recount stories know what they are talking about? In everyday storytelling, we may as listeners challenge what we hear. How do you know that? Who told you? Are you sure? I was told a very different story by your friend Alice—who am I to believe? When it's a story told in a court of law, it is supposed to come from a direct witness: the law rejects "hearsay evidence," stories passed on from others. Yet to credit a witness unthinkingly may be naive as well: recollections, even of recent events, can be distorted; eyewitnesses can make grave errors. If we are to believe the story we are hearing, we need to be convinced of the good faith and reliability of the narrator. He or she needs to persuade us: this is the way it happened. We know from literature as well as life that unreliable narrators can at times be charming and seductive, even that the non-truth they tell can have a certain value. But we seek to discriminate the trustworthy from the suspect.

In our reading of novels, we're most often used to either an impersonal narration that speaks in the third person or else a first-person discourse. There are many variations along this spectrum: third-person narrators who may be highly characterized, or on the contrary, seemingly neutral or invisible; those who may appear to know everything about their characters and world ("omniscience," as we generally call it); or those from whom such knowledge may be partly hidden. There are even second-person narrators, seemingly narrators speaking to themselves—or to us. And first-person narrators can be single or plural, smart or stupid, transparent or obfuscatory, straight shooters or liars. Fiction gives us access to other minds, and over the centuries it has tended to do so ever more fluidly, moving from the relative formality of the letter, for instance—a firsthand account offered to a listener or reader within the text—to psycho-narration or narrated monologue, following the consciousness of one or more characters.[1] When we are privy to a given mind it's infrequent that this mind will know fully what's going on in another—it must undertake the sometimes arduous business of trying to read other minds, a skill we use and need for social survival, and one of the learned pleasures of reading novels.[2] If mind reading were simple and straightforward, we would not have the detective story, for instance—which extols penetrating mind reading but puts stumbling blocks in its way.

Readers learn to deal with the most experimental and subtle ways that tellers use to make us want to hear them out, and to make us believe, intellectually and emotionally, in what they tell. We can rationalize some inconsistencies in point of view, chronology, and continuity.[3] But in works that aspire to a generally realist presentation of life, there would seem to be at least one inviolable prohibition: you can't recount your own death. "I am dead" is, for the human species, an impossible utterance. Edgar Allan Poe plays upon this limit in his story "The Facts in the Case of M. Valdemar," in which a man who has just died is brought back to life in an experiment with mesmerism—only to pronounce that impossible phrase, "I am dead," and then to decompose rapidly. Other examples that come to mind are explicitly marked as deviations from standard narration: Alice Sebold's *The Lovely Bones* is told by a narrator gone to heaven; William Faulkner's *As I Lay Dying* gives a voice to the dead Addie Bundren, but it's not clear whether she is speaking or whether the narrator, who enters multiple consciousnesses in the course of the book, speaks on her behalf. The age-old poetic technique of apostrophe can often result in the speech of the dead—but clearly it is in a tongue lent to them by the poet.

Yet Paula Hawkins's *The Girl on the Train*, a best-selling novel from 2015 that went on to become a popular film, does the unthinkable: one of its main characters recounts her own death. *The Girl on the Train* is focused primarily in the mind and observations of alcoholic Rachel, who from her commuter train window looks out at the house in Witney, near London, that she used to inhabit with Tom, now married to Anna, and the nearby house of Scott and Megan, behind which she sees Megan, who later mysteriously disappears, carrying on with her therapist Kamal. The premise of the novel is somewhat detectivelike, perhaps with a nod to Alfred Hitchcock's *Rear Window*: Rachel, from her limited view through the train window, needs to figure out what's happening among the other characters, including Tom, to whom she is still emotionally attached. She goes to Witney, shows up unwelcomed at Tom and Anna's, at Scott's, at Kamal's office, and one evening when she is staggeringly drunk she witnesses something in the railway underpass. It's only the retrospective elucidation of this alcohol-clouded memory that will allow her to understand that Tom has killed Megan—pregnant by him—thereby solving the mystery of her disappearance. The novel is told in successive chapters in which each of the principals—Rachel, Anna, Megan—recounts events from her point of view.

Megan's final chapter describes her death at Tom's hand:

> He's coming towards me. He has something in his hand.
>
> I've fallen. I must have slipped. Hit my head on something. I think I'm going to be sick. Everything is red. I can't get up.
>
> One for sorrow, two for joy, three for a girl … Three for a girl. I'm stuck on three, I just can't get any further. My head is thick with sounds, my mouth thick with blood. Three for a girl. I can hear the magpies—they're laughing, mocking me, a raucous cackling. A tiding. Bad tidings. I can see them now, black against the sun. Not the birds, something else. Someone's coming. Someone is speaking to me. *Now look. Now look at what you made me do.*[4]

One may or may not find this a plausible imagining of what it is to die—it's close to how one may feel after an accident—but it is impossible as a reported utterance. It violates the rules of perspective—of partial, limited visions—set up by this novel itself, and the larger rules of what you might call novelistic evidence. The narratologist Shlomith Rimmon-Kenan notes that an "external focalizer" (like the so-called omniscient narrator) can in theory know everything about the world within the novel, but the "knowledge of an internal focalizer … is restricted by definition: being a part of the represented world, he cannot know everything about it."[5] Who was there to report this interior monologue? How was it written down? All the other instances of narrative in *The Girl on the Train* are rationalized, justified. This one stands in neverland.[6]

Compare Tolstoy's *The Death of Ivan Ilyich*, a harrowing account of the end of life that claims to record a dying person's final sensations and thoughts:

"It is finished!" someone said over him.

He heard those words and repeated them in his soul. "Death is finished," he said to himself. "It is no more."

He drew in air, stopped at mid breath, stretched out, and died.[7]

Tolstoy's intimacy with Ivan Ilyich's dying thoughts is purchased by his stance of narrative omniscience. He makes no pretense to limited perspective, but on the contrary presents himself as just about as all-knowing as the deity. Another classic example comes at the end of Flaubert's novella *A Simple Heart*, as the servant Félicité passes from life to death and confounds her stuffed parrot with the Holy Ghost:

The azure vapor of incense rose to Félicité's room. She opened her nostrils, taking it in with a mystic sensuality; then closed her eyelids. Her lips were smiling. The movements of her heart slowed one by one, more uncertain each time, softer, as a fountain runs dry, as an echo fades away; and, when she exhaled her last breath, she thought she saw, in the opening heavens, a gigantic parrot, soaring over her head.[8]

Flaubert's narrator daringly takes us virtually over the threshold from life to death. But it is of course that narrator, not Félicité herself, who reports this ultimate moment. It is an entirely different matter to claim, in a thriller that develops through the drama of different minds limited by their incomplete perspectives on the world, to recount the climactic moment in one of those minds. That mind is now nonexistent, and her voice silenced. It makes no sense.

Why do I feel offended by what Paula Hawkins has done? Another recent novel, Emily St. John Mandel's *The Glass Hotel* (2020), reports the heroine's death by drowning in the first person and, I think, gets away with it: Vincent's death (yes, Vincent is a woman) evokes the traditional notion that the dying, especially the drowning, experience an instant replay of their lives, and that's what we have here, in a kind of dreamy register that is unbound from any requirements of point of view or fidelity to the real. To enter the realm of magical realism gets you off the hook. But *The Girl on the Train* establishes itself in the tradition of the whodunit and the psychological thriller. Recall that initial premise of what can be seen from the train window as the train slows and stops at Witney. James Wood has declared realism to be the "broad central language of the novel," the language that brought the novel into being and continues to serve as its dominant expected convention.[9] We open a novel in the initial expectation that it will conform to the conventions of our lives within time, space, and gravity. It's free to set its own rules, but the reader will need to be taught these. If it is going to present itself as a Hitchcockian thriller, the rules are too well known to be violated with impunity.

Is the point I am making of any importance? Certainly Megan's self-reported death did not damage the popularity of *The Girl on the Train*. Yet its violation of narrative perspective and reporting does suggest large questions about knowing and narrative. There is a long tradition of worry about the source of what narrators have to tell us, especially in matters of intimate personal emotions. From the early years of the novel, as it sought acceptance by establishing its good faith, the question of how the story has come to be known and told has been crucial. Take for instance the case of the *Letters of a Portuguese Nun* (*Lettres portugaises*), published in 1669 and preceded by an unsigned "Note to the Reader" that claims: "I have found the means, with much care and trouble, to recover an accurate copy of five Portuguese Letters that were written to a noble gentleman who was serving in Portugal."[10] This presentation managed to convince most readers over the next three centuries that the heartbreaking letters from the nun abandoned by her lover were authentic. The attribution of the *Lettres* to its author, Gabriel de Guilleragues, was established only around 1950.

As Guilleragues's twentieth-century editor put it, the "public requires that it be tricked"—that is, tricked into believing the story to be "real."[11] Readers display a wish to be deluded into thinking the stuff of novels a "true story," as when Denis Diderot in praising Samuel Richardson dreams of having bought an old château and while walking through its rooms finding an old chest; then, having broken into it, he discovered pell-mell the letters of Clarissa and Pamela.[12] After reading a few of them he feels impelled to arrange them by date, distressed if he finds any missing. Diderot is not a naive reader; what he describes here is wanting the novelistic illusion.

Looking back to other novels early in the European tradition, such as the anonymous *Lazarillo de Tormes* (1554) and Daniel Defoe's *Robinson Crusoe* (1719), they strike us as deeply concerned in their themes and plots with elements of epistemology: They crucially think about how we know, even if it be the simplest means of survival. They feature a world of empirical experimentation and learning. Lazaro must learn to survive in a harsh world in which he starts out with nothing. As a blind beggar's boy, he learns tricks in order to get food, drink, and money: sneaking a straw into his master's wine jar, for instance, and concealing coins in his mouth. When the tricks are discovered, retribution is swift and painful—and a lesson in how to evade future detection, to turn the tables. The castaway Robinson has long stood as the paradigm of learning to survive by one's wits, opposing human ingenuity to a hostile environment, creating the basic elements of civilization in the wilderness. Learning to know the signs that allow you to survive and prosper comes, later in the novel, to be emblematized by the enigmatic footprint in the sand, which will lead to the discovery of the cannibals, then eventually to the rescue and enlistment of Friday, and finally to rescue from the island. Already Sherlock Holmes is on the horizon.

When we reach *Clarissa* and the inception of the modern novel of inner experience, we find Samuel Richardson puzzling out the problem of fiction and illusion. To Bishop Warburton, who supplied a preface to *Clarissa*, Richardson writes:

> Will you, good Sir, allow me to mention, that I could wish that the *Air* of Genuiness [*sic*] had been kept up, tho' I want not the Letters to be *thought* genuine; only so far kept up, I mean, as that they should not prefatically be owned *not* to be genuine: and this for fear of weakening their Influence where any of them are aimed to be exemplary; as well as to avoid hurting that kind of Historical Faith which Fiction itself is generally read with, tho' we know it to be Fiction.[13]

Richardson's somewhat self-contradictory sentence captures well the willing suspension of disbelief that readers bring to novels, not necessarily from naiveté or stupidity but because that is part of the intellectual and emotional pleasure of reading a novel. Even though you know it to be fiction you need to submit to its simulations of the real. And for those simulations to work, the game must be played fully and wholly: even your prefacer should observe the rules.

Many novels in the eighteenth century go to elaborate lengths to claim their "real" source, in the kind of trunk-full-of-letters scenario imagined by Diderot reading Richardson. Defoe in his author's preface to *The Fortunes and Misfortunes of the Famous Moll Flanders* (1722) claims his authorial role has been simply to clean up Moll's language, more fit for Newgate Prison than for a polite audience: "The pen employed in finishing her story, and making it what you now see it to be, has had no little difficulty to put it into a dress fit to be seen, and to make it speak language fit to be read."[14] But the story itself is Moll's (if you want to believe so). The prolific Abbé Prévost, best known for his *Manon Lescaut* (which really is the final volume of his very long *Memoirs of a Man of Quality* [*Mémoires d'un homme de qualité qui s'est retiré du monde*]) but author of many another work as well, is ever concerned with the question of how his narrators come by the information they convey to readers: manuscripts are found and translated, oral tales are transcribed, the author is presented as the simple "editor" of the material. Marivaux's *The Life of Marianne* (*La Vie de Marianne*) opens with the story of how the manuscript of Marianne's first-person account of her adventures came to the "editor." Rousseau in his preface in dialogue form to his epistolary novel *The New Heloise* (*Julie; ou La nouvelle Héloïse*) refuses to say categorically whether or not the letters he has published are real—and there is ample evidence in the fan mail sent to the author that many readers insisted on believing that they were, demanding to meet the real-life versions of Julie and her lover, Saint-Preux.

The novelist who plays most self-consciously with questions of knowing and narrating is in fact Diderot, who in *The Nun* (*La Religieuse*) creates an elaborate trompe-l'oeil to trick his friend the Marquis de Croismare into believing that Sister Suzanne, the persecuted nun at the heart of the novel, is real and in need of succor in her attempts to renounce a forced vocation and escape abusive treatment in her convent. What began as ruse became a novel, one that convinced its intended audience of its truth-to-life. Then in *Jacques the Fatalist and His Master* (*Jacques le fataliste et son maître*), Diderot undertook (somewhat in the spirit of Laurence Sterne's *Tristram Shandy*, but more radically) a novel that constantly questions its fictional status and the role of author in its arbitrary unfolding. Jacques the valet believes that the plots of life proceed according to the inexorable script of "*le grand rouleau*," a scroll unfurled in heaven, whereas his master forever needles him into considering the arbitrariness of such a view. The fatalism of the title is that of novelistic form itself.

My examples so far are largely French: eighteenth-century French novelists were much concerned with the epistemological issues of narrative, perhaps the legacy of Descartes but also certainly because of the arbitrary and sometimes severe censorship of novels at the time, which placed an incentive on claiming that one was not the author of the work.[15] Evading the censor led to elaborate games for covering one's tracks or, more playfully, injecting the problem of truth and falsehood with a killing dose of ambiguity. See, as best instance, the prefatory material of Choderlos de Laclos's *Les Liaisons dangereuses*, where a lengthy editor's preface explains how he has obtained and ordered the letters while refraining from edits that would have improved and unified their differing styles (underlining the author's skill at writing letters in many different idioms). But this preface has already been disestablished by a Notice from the Publisher, who has reason to doubt the authenticity of the letters and suspects that the book may be merely a novel. The reason for this suspicion: the manners displayed in the book are so vile one cannot accept that they belong to the present day, when Enlightenment has made all men honest and all women modest and virtuous. No doubt, the publisher notes, the author has transposed material from another time and place to present-day France, and in the process made his story wholly lack verisimilitude. Laclos's ironies cut in many directions, thoroughly scrambling the fact/fiction divide.

Early in the next century, you find an elaborate example of framing in Benjamin Constant's novel *Adolphe* (1816). A first narrator is detained at an inn because of a spring flood that makes roads impassable; there he meets a bored and embittered man who, when travel again becomes possible, leaves behind at the inn a small casket that contains a manuscript. The first narrator sends the manuscript to a friend who lived in the same (unidentified) town as its writer, and after reading it this friend decides that it should be published as a useful example of how not to live your life. At just about the same moment, Mary Shelley's *Frankenstein* (1818) frames its story of scientific overreaching and monstrous creation with an exchange of letters between the polar explorer Robert Walton and his sister Mrs. Saville. The letters recount how Walton sighted the Monster and then met its creator, Victor Frankenstein, in pursuit across the ice floes. As in the case of *Adolphe*, the framing material wants to authenticate the reality of the embedded tale (plural in the case of *Frankenstein*, since Victor's narrative will also enclose the Monster's), to say something like: I, like you the reader, am only the recipient of this material. However bizarre this story may appear, I have invented nothing. Or, as a couple of decades later, in 1835, Honoré de Balzac will announce on the first page of *Père Goriot*: "All is true." Balzac's phrase is in English in the original, in honor of a performance of Shakespeare he had seen under that title, and maybe also in homage to the English novel. To be sure, readers were not obliged in these cases to accept the illusionistic presentation: all this "paratextual" material may most of all signal the entry into a fictional world and a solicitation of the reader's attention to the kind of immersive reading it demands.[16]

Megan's account of her own death in *The Girl on the Train* reminds me of one of the most problematic cases of narrating in the nineteenth century, Victor Hugo's *The Last Day of a Condemned Man* (*Le Dernier Jour d'un condamné*, 1829), which takes on the challenge of recounting in the first person the last day of a convict sentenced to die on the guillotine. Hugo scrupulously motivates the convict's narration throughout: he is writing a diary of his final thoughts, self-consciously reflecting on what it feels like to be on the verge of extinction: an *I* who knows that by the end of that day he will no longer be able to say *I*. Most of the diary is written in his prison cell. When he is transferred in the afternoon to the Hôtel de Ville, outside of which stands the guillotine, he asks his guard to remove his handcuffs and bring him paper and ink to record his very last thoughts, written out with hands still numb from being bound. However implausible it might seem that the gendarme would fulfill such a request, the reader at least detects Hugo's wish to explain and to justify the source of the narrative report here. The novel comes to its end while the condemned man is writing his ultimate words with the capitalized: FOUR O'CLOCK. The moment of execution has arrived; there will be no further words.

Hugo wants to represent the anguished consciousness of a man on the verge of execution—of literally having the thinking and speaking part of him severed from the body—by getting inside that mind. It's effective, and it makes his plea against the death penalty all the more potent. Nonetheless, readers may find it hard to accept the artifice of the final pages written just before the convict is taken outside to the guillotine. But it interests me that Hugo is acutely aware that he must justify the continuation of the first-person narration to the very foot of the scaffold—and he does not, unlike Paula Hawkins, carry it further, to the reflections of the convict as the blade descends on his neck. That would strike us as absurd, as Megan's death scene also should. If it doesn't, it must mean that we have given up any concern with how we know what we are being told. And maybe in the era of fake news and Facebook and memes generated from the dark web, that is the case.

It's true that over the course of the nineteenth century novelists worried less about justifying the sources of their narrators' and their characters' knowledge. It is as if the genre had established itself firmly enough that it was largely exempt from the anxieties displayed in the previous century, when the novel was trying to demonstrate its legitimacy, often by denying that it was a novel (or romance), insisting on its fidelity to empirical truth. Austen, Dickens, Balzac, Eliot, Tolstoy, Flaubert on the whole make the assumption that it is best simply to plunge into telling the story without prefatory justifications. And their novels tend (with many exceptions) toward what we usually call omniscient narration, though that catchall term obscures the many variations in what narrators know and don't, what they reveal and conceal, the extent to which they understand all the minds at work in the story they have to tell. If, for instance, the narrator of Stendhal's *The Red and the Black* (*Le Rouge et le noir*) appears to have access to all his characters' inner thoughts, even those of which they are themselves largely unaware, he also admits at times that he doesn't understand the mind and actions of his protagonist, Julien Sorel, whom he both censures and admires for what is least predictable in his behavior. As the century progressed, novels tended more and more to enter their characters' minds by way of psycho-narration, following a character's thoughts, or more radically narrated monologue, *style indirect libre*, where the narration moves without overt marking into a character's consciousness and proceeds as if this were itself the narrative—as increasingly it is, from Flaubert to James Joyce to Virginia Woolf. In the critical reflection on his novels carried out by Henry James in his prefaces to the New York Edition of his work we have the first sustained commentary on point of view, limitation of vision, and the understanding of narrative consciousness in the history of the genre. The twentieth century will come to look more like the eighteenth in its worries about narrative epistemology.

Cheating in the composition of novels may seem acceptable if you take the whole business of creating an alternate world and the imaginary beings who inhabit it to be a sleight of hand. But to cheat so that it becomes evident to readers that they are being treated as unintelligent and unaware won't do, unless you are dealing with readers who wish to be stupefied. Consider in this context the detective story, perhaps the most rule bound of narrative genres. The composition of a detective story is comparable to the writing of a sonnet: if you fail to observe the rules, it's just not a sonnet. The detective story is of course considerably looser in its rules than the sonnet, but if it doesn't engage the reader in the search for clues and the pursuit of a solution to the initial enigma—the crime—it won't read as detective fiction. In the series that did the most to establish our expectations of the genre, Arthur Conan Doyle's tales of Sherlock Holmes, standard procedure dictates that the detective go over the crime scene, most often with an interlocutor such as Watson or an obtuse police inspector, to whom he reports his findings. He follows the steps of the malefactor while the reader follows his steps. The most striking example may be "The Musgrave Ritual," in which Holmes understands the apparently opaque document read aloud by each Musgrave scion upon coming of age, known as the Ritual, as the instructions of a treasure map. He follows the clues hidden in the Ritual at Hurlstone, the Musgrave estate, and in doing so finds evidence that he is walking a path earlier marked out by the criminal, the butler Brunton. The detective repeats the steps of his predecessor—and this leads to the solution.[17]

"I'll tell you what I did first, and how I came to do it afterwards," says Holmes as he begins his final elucidation in "The Naval Treaty."[18] That may stand as an emblem of how the classic detective story proceeds. When the game is played fairly, the story presents us with all the facts, and the detective will pick those that are truly clues and enchain them into the narrative that leads to the solution. Readers often complain that they can't really perform the detection themselves: that there are missing links, observations on the part of the detective that go unreported. Some readers claim to read detective fiction backwards, starting with the solution and then reading for the plot to make sure that the clues have all been furnished to the reader. The writer who omits necessary information is judged to have abused the genre. Yet it seems to me that what we really seek in the detective story is the sense of discovering a solution from intelligence working on a recalcitrant reality, claiming a victory of mind over matter, wresting order from the apparent chaos represented by crime. The important thing is that we feel we are part of the game, that we might have exercised the observational and intellectual acuity of Sherlock Holmes and reached the solution. A book such as *The Girl on the Train* (which I am of course using as whipping girl: there would surely be other examples as well) does not play its game fairly.

The detective story, in its very limitations and conventionality, its particularly rule-bound ways of representing the world, points us to the complex issues of perspective and knowing discussed in Henry James's prefaces. James in fact sets himself up as a kind of detective going over again the ground of his published novels, tracing their development from the original "germ of suggestion" that set him thinking about a novel, to sketching it out and then undertaking its creation. He is not always the most reliable reader of his own work: he makes claims about what is going on in his novels that don't always correspond to the reader's experience of them. To claim, for instance, that Rowland Mallet's consciousness alone is central to *Roderick Hudson* seems mistaken; his assignment of Book 1 of *The Golden Bowl* exclusively to the consciousness of Prince Amerigo, and Book 2 to the princess, Maggie Verver, makes mincemeat of Colonel and Fanny Assingham, whose choral commentary not only presents crucial past events for the reader but also interprets the present and constructs possible futures.

James's urge to tidy up his own narrative strategies does, however, show him rereading his novels in the spirit of a detective. In that same preface to *The Golden Bowl*, he begins by noting, once again but yet more forcefully, "my preference for dealing with my subject-matter, for 'seeing my story,' through the opportunity and the sensibility of some more or less detached, some not strictly involved, though thoroughly interested and intelligent, witness or reporter, some person who contributes to the case mainly a certain amount of criticism and interpretation of it." In reviewing his work, he finds again and again that he has not given "my own impersonal account of the affair in hand" but rather "my account of somebody's impression if it." And then: "the terms of this person's access to it and estimate of it contributing thus by some fine little law to intensification of interest." Crucial here I think is James's mention that point of view very much involves the question of how that witness gained access to the story and what he or she thought of it. Access and report for James inherently increase the dramatic interest of the subject. "Anything, in short, I now reflect, must always have seemed to me better—better for the process and the effect of representation, my irrepressible ideal—than the mere muffled majesty of irresponsible 'authorship.'"[19]

A key if baffling phrase. Why is "authorship" irresponsible?

James's stricture here seems to be at once aesthetic and ethical, claiming that authorship, by which I take it he means a traditional all-knowing narrator, eliminates from composition the more interesting effect gained by limiting point of view to someone who bears a personal relation to the story, giving us not only the story but the story of the story, so to speak. And that mere authorship not only fails to give this extra dimension of interest to the story but betokens a kind of mental laziness that fails in the high task of the novelist: to show the moral universe in all its complexity. This is of course an idiosyncratic claim, since there are there are plenty of novelists who do just fine with traditional omniscient narration. Yet James does set a standard and issue a challenge that many in his wake have responded to. The multiple perspectives of Joyce's *Ulysses* and Woolf's *The Waves*, the radical narrative splintering in Faulkner's *The Sound and the Fury* and *Absalom, Absalom!*, the layered, ever more complex manipulation of plot in John le Carré's *The Spy Who Came In from the Cold*, to take a very few arbitrary examples, show novelists working out possible consequences of an attention to how stories come to be known and told and retold by those who stand in relation to them, and for whom sometimes these questions may be a matter of life and death. James makes the act of telling, including the listening to and making sense of narrative, a central drama of narrative fiction. There is no single right way of making good on James's standard and his challenge. But he illuminates a proud tradition in which narrative strives both to absorb us in the story and make us think about how stories come to us and work on us. Surely he is right that such reflection on the transmission and reception of stories matters in the creation of significant fictions of life. Anything else is laziness.

James creates stories within stories by making the motive of storytelling and story listening—reception—a crucial question. In *The Golden Bowl*, the question is essentially: Who controls the narrative? If throughout Book 1 it is the adulterous couple, the prince and Charlotte Stant, who both conceal their relationship and present it deceptively to others, in Book 2 Maggie self-consciously and decisively wrests narrative authority from them, refusing overt recognition to the adultery plot, overwriting it with the reaffirmation of her marriage and the banishment of Charlotte, along with Adam Verver, to American City. Think also of James's wildest experiment in the drama of narrative creation, motivation, and control: *The Sacred Fount.* Here the unnamed but very participant narrator/observer exercises his intelligence and imagination at an English country house weekend by postulating relationships among the other guests. His interpretation of who is sexually engaged with whom is based on the axiom—once postulated it is never questioned—that in all couples one member is drinking from the "sacred fount" of the other, gaining strength and youth while the partner withers, ages, is depleted. Any modification in his understanding of who is with whom inevitably entails other changes, all based on this same axiom, which works as an algorithm, generating patterns of partnering. When toward the end his confidante, Grace Brissenden, who has seemed to participate in his storytelling strategy tells him he is simply crazy, his initial collapse is followed by an attempt to rebuild the narrative structure by factoring in Grace herself and the relationship she is anxious to conceal in rejecting his narrative principle. The novel leaves us more or less nowhere. It's a kind of self-consuming artifact that has invited us to play the game of narrative construction and motivation without furnishing a result. It's a precursor of those twentieth-century failed detective stories like Julio Cortázar's "Blow-Up" and Alain Robbe-Grillet's *The Voyeur*—detective stories in which it's uncertain there has even been a crime, let alone an investigation and solution.

Let me turn here to Faulkner's *Absalom, Absalom!* as a novel in which coming to know how the story came to be known is at once crucial to the power of the story and also supremely questionable: essential knowledge seemingly is hidden from the reader. Though the needed knowledge may indeed be there, if not in plain view at least detectable. *Absalom, Absalom!* turns on a number of important enigmas; solving them and so achieving an intelligible relation to the past is largely what the narrative is about. For the two young men, Quentin Compson and Shreve McCannon, who are caught up in discussion about the story of the past in their freezing dormitory room at Harvard, the most fraught enigma concerns Henry Sutpen's killing of Charles Bon, his best friend and his sister's fiancé. Over the course of their investigatory narrative, working from what Quentin was told by his father—who in turn learned some of it from his own father, General Compson, who befriended Thomas Sutpen—and by Rosa Coldfield, and what he experienced himself a few months earlier on visiting Sutpen's plantation (Sutpen's Hundred), the reasons for Henry's shooting of Bon at the gate to his father's house keep changing as the two young men build on what they think they know and discard what has come to seem false or misleading. At first it is alleged—this is General Compson's version—that the problem was the discovery that Bon was already married—though in a morganatic marriage without legal substance—to an octoroon woman in New Orleans. Bon is thus an "intending bigamist" in his courtship of Judith Sutpen. But that doesn't seem sufficient motivation to Quentin or his father. Next, there is the discovery that Bon is in fact Sutpen's son by his first marriage, thus Henry and Judith's half brother. So added to the bigamy is incest. Yet even that doesn't seem to explain Henry's murderous act, especially since he harbors incestuous desires for Judith himself. Still later in the narrative emerges the decisive fact, hitherto hidden: that Bon's mother, whom Thomas Sutpen married in Haiti, had Negro blood. That led to Sutpen's repudiation of her and then his later marriage to Ellen Coldfield, Rosa's sister, mother of Judith and Henry. This discovery offers a key to explaining what happened between Henry and Charles Bon, the white and the part-Black sons. It is powerful enough to call up from the past—or create in the imagination?—a crucial scene from near the end of the Civil War, in 1865, as the Confederate army retreats toward Richmond. Colonel Sutpen summons Henry to his tent to explain why Judith must not be allowed to marry Bon: *"He must not marry her, Henry. His mother's father told me that her mother had been a Spanish woman. I believed him; it was not until after he was born that I found out that his mother was part negro."*[20] This overt statement finally gives Quentin and Shreve the hermeneutic clue they need to understand the tragic epic of the Sutpen family.

But wait (as Shreve repeatedly says to Quentin as they get deeper into the story they are constructing together): Where does this certainty come from? Not, it appears, from any information handed down from the past but from Quentin's own observation the night he went out to Sutpen's Hundred with Rosa Coldfield in the fall of

1909, just before his departure for Harvard. It's Shreve who zeroes in on the problematic source of Quentin's information:

> "Your father," Shreve said . . . "If he knew all this, what was his reason for telling you that the trouble between Henry and Bon was the octoroon woman?"
>
> "He didn't know it then. Grandfather didn't tell him all of it either, like Sutpen never told Grandfather quite all of it."
>
> "Then who did tell him?"
>
> "I did." Quentin did not move, did not look up while Shreve watched him. "The day after we—after that night when we—"
>
> "Oh," Shreve said. "After you and the old aunt. I see."

How Quentin learned what he did during that visit to Sutpen's Hundred is made more explicit a few pages later:

> "Your old man," Shreve said. "When your grandfather was telling this to him, he didn't know any more what your grandfather was talking about than your grandfather knew what the demon [Sutpen] was talking about when the demon told it to him, did he? And when your old man told it to you, you wouldn't have known what anybody was talking about if you hadn't been out there and seen Clytie. Is that right?"
>
> "Yes," Quentin said.

Which is to say, reading in the margins of what is made explicit, that the decisive clue to the story comes retroactively, from Quentin's meeting with Clytie (Clytemnestra), who is Sutpen's daughter by one of his slaves. Seeing Clytie, he witnesses the Sutpen features in a Black face, and this triggers his recognition that miscegenation is the only workable explanation for Henry's shooting of Bon.[21] He has probably seen Clytie in Jefferson before, but now it is with a new attention, in the old house where he also meets Henry, the dying survivor from the epic past. In a novel that turns on the uncertainty of historical explanation as well as the need for it, no interpretation can be offered as final. It is part of the honesty of the novel to refuse finalities. Yet the narrative convinces me that Quentin's eyewitnessing of Clytie offers the best key to the enigmas the novel presents. To "see Clytie" is to witness the trace of miscegenation running though the Sutpen family—the trace of an irony, since it is what Sutpen most wished to avoid in his search for social legitimacy. It "explains" where earlier hypotheses did not. And Quentin's eyewitness report may justify Quentin's taking over of the narration from his father and grandfather: even though he is a belated narrator in relation to the Sutpen epic, he knows more than those temporally closer to the events. He has made himself into the best detective, tracking down the explanatory principles of the story.

In Faulkner, that "mere muffled majesty of irresponsible 'authorship'" that James deplored has been decisively renounced: authorship becomes a central issue in the drama of the novel. Quentin in dialogue with Shreve takes over the telling of the story from his father and grandfather, and in doing so demands that readers, too, engage with the always open question of narrative authority. There may never be epistemological certainty in this novel; what we have is a best guess at an explanation. Freud, in his late essay "Constructions in Analysis," says that the search to recover the past in the psychoanalytic dialogue between patient and analyst may never recover a verifiable past history. Sometimes, all you have is a construction of the past "which achieves the same therapeutic result as a recaptured memory."[22] Narrative may have to make do with "what must have happened" rather than any assured truth. Narrative epistemology, pursued with integrity, gives us only the best possible mimesis of what we know of the world: a story that is persuasive, that makes us understand how things might have happened. It doesn't delude us about our knowledge of the past in the manner of *The Girl on the Train.* It rather makes that knowing a problem and a drama.

Against the plot of narrative knowing in many a story lies the weight of *unknowing*: the sinister power of nescience. In James's *The Wings of the Dove*, when Milly Theale at last sheds her blindness to the relationship of Merton Densher and Kate Croy, she dies. A kind of willful ignorance is at the heart of James's late novella *The Beast in the Jungle*: John Marcher's blindness becomes a killing narcissism, destroying first May Bartram and then himself. An early and compelling example can be found in what is often called the first psychological novel in the Western tradition, Madame de Lafayette's *The Princess of Clèves* (*La Princesse de Clèves*, 1678), which turns on the extraordinary confession of wife to husband—the princess to the prince—that she loves and is loved by another man but will never give in to that passion. When her confession becomes known at the court, and the other man is named as the Duc de Nemours, husband and wife confront one another over who has betrayed their secret. Both deny having done so, and it had clearly been in the interest of both not to reveal it. Each believes the other is guilty. There is a crucial impasse in knowing that will eventually cause the death of the prince. In fact the crucial confession was overheard by the eavesdropping Nemours, who has not been able to resist revealing his own starring role in it. Neither the prince nor the princess knows that, however: they are ignorant of what is a matter of life or death to them both. The prince dies from his ignorance; the princess retreats from the court. Their epistemological impotence appears to undo the elaborate games of penetrating disguises on which the court is based. The novel turns on this failure to know in a world where knowing is what life is all about. Ignorance is mortal.

Eavesdropping itself, crucial to the plot of knowledge and nescience in *The Princess of Clèves*, has a distinguished novelistic career.[23] After Madame de Lafayette's novel, the most sensational example that comes to mind is the moment in Wilkie Collins's *The Woman in White* when Marian Halcombe climbs out her bedroom window onto the roof to overhear Sir Percival Glyde and Count Fosco conceiving the elaborate plot that will dominate the rest of the novel—an episode that also results in Marian's drenching in a sudden rainfall, hence her illness, which in turn gives Fosco the opportunity to invade her bedroom and read the journal in which she has tracked her suspicions about the plotters. There is also a great and crucial moment of eavesdropping in Robert Louis Stevenson's *Treasure Island*, when Jim Hawkins, hidden in the bottom of the apple barrel, hears Long John Silver and his confederates plotting their mutiny. And there's a complex instance at the outset of Marcel Proust's *Sodom and Gomorrah*, about halfway through *In Search of Lost Time*, when the young Marcel, from a concealed vantage point on the staircase, witnesses the encounter of the Baron de Charlus and the tailor Jupien and begins to discover the hidden world of homosexuality that will so radically alter his perspectives on society and eros. If eavesdropping may suffer from a certain implausibility as a device, its use can precisely justify the acquisition of needed narrative knowledge. It may be morally dubious and a tired convention, but it has great cognitive value.

Narrative seems among other things nearly always to be bound up with questions of knowing; it is a cognitive instrument. Hayden White suggests that the Indo-European root of the word "narrative" refers to knowing, which might in turn imply that originally narrative is "wisdom literature," which tells of our origins, of where we and the world came from.[24] Carlo Ginzburg's huntsman's paradigm ties the beginnings of narrative to the huntsman's lore. The linking of traces, clues, and incidents into a narrative—that of the passage of an animal, for instance—suggests that narrative originally and always represents an act of cognition. That in turn has meant that questions of how we learn what we claim to know has been crucial to the novel. If I have been harsh in criticism of *The Girl on the Train* it's because it seems worth insisting on the real work that the novel at its best can accomplish. If we let ourselves be seduced by the sloppiness of something like *The Girl on the Train*, the sky will not fall. Yet since the novel has become the overwhelmingly dominant form of our modernity, it may be valuable to keep reminding ourselves that it need not be sloppy, that an important part of its criticism of life is to alert us to how we know and make sense of life's stories.

3. The Teller, the Told, the Difference It Makes

TALES ARE TOLD FOR MANY REASONS, to listeners present or absent, and usually to make a point. The breakthrough work done by sociolinguists William Labov and Joshua Waletzky in the 1960s on oral narratives of personal experience recounted by inner-city teenagers brought this powerfully home. These oral stories tend to contain a moment of "evaluation" in which the speaker reflects on the meaning or the lesson of his experience—implicitly, on why he is telling this tale.[1] It may be easy to forget when reading a novel, a form generally consumed in solitude, that we are its addressees, that the author has imagined the reading and even readership of this novel, that it is an attempt at communication. One that may very well go awry: Plato notes in his *Phaedrus* that the problem with written texts is that they roam around everywhere, promiscuously, and it's impossible to know how they will be received, interpreted, acted upon.[2] The oral storyteller, on the other hand, can gauge audience reaction, respond to questions or skeptical looks or bored body language. Many writers in the age of writing and print appear to look back upon the era of oral storytelling with nostalgia, as a less fallen age of communication and fellowship. European folktales, for instance—stories that traditionally united family generations and village clans during long winter evenings close to the fire—began to be transcribed, collected, and preserved in such books as the *Kinder- und Hausmärchen* (Children's and Household Tales) that the Brothers Grimm first published in 1812, just as they were disappearing from popular oral culture.

Oral storytelling puts live people in a situation of exchange. As the folklorist John Niles states in his book *Homo Narrans*: "Oral performance has a corporeality about it, a sensible, somatic quality, that derives from the bodily presence of performers and listeners."[3] There is a famous evocation of this somatic quality in the preface to another nineteenth-century attempt to preserve an oral tradition, Richard Burton's *The Book of the Thousand Nights and a Night*, which describes the scene of a Bedouin encampment where he tells the tales he has selected:

> As the giant grey shadow rises slowly in the East and the vagueness of evening waxes wan in the West and night comes on without a shade of gloaming, and, as it were, with a single stride, and Earth looks old, and pallid, and cold, *alt, kalt,* and *ungestalt*, the spectre of her former self, the camp forgathers. The Shaykhs and "white-beards" of the tribe gravely take their places, sitting with outspread skirts like hillocks on the plain, as the Arabs say, around the campfire, whilst I reward their hospitality and secure its continuance by reading or reciting a few pages of their favourite tales. The women and children stand motionless as silhouettes outside the ring; and all are breathless with attention: they seem to drink in the words with eyes and mouth as well as with ears.[4]

Burton evokes a kind of authenticity of story and its reception that haunts later narrators, an utter absorption in the told that classic authors of children's literature, from Robert Louis Stevenson to Edith Nesbit, at times succeed in reviving.

A number of nineteenth-century novelists re-create fictionally the situation of oral storytelling. Take Balzac, for example, probably the first novelist to understand fully the implications of the new print and publishing culture in which he wrote. His novel *Lost Illusions* (*Illusions Perdues*) turns on of the fate of the writer, who first conceives himself as a poet, when he enters the machinery of journalism, publicity, and production that was emerging in France during the 1820s and '30s. *Lost Illusions*, as Georg Lukács described it, is the "tragi-comic epic of the capitalization of spirit," which records literature becoming a commodity.[5] Balzac was prescient enough to try to gain control of the means and modes of production by buying a printshop and a type foundry. They went bankrupt under his management, but his idea was not wrong. He sensed the coming of what the contemporary critic Sainte-Beuve would in 1839 label "industrial literature," in which longer novels, often published in serial form in the daily newspaper, led to lower newspaper subscription costs, paid advertising, and venal book reviewing. Literature was becoming popular (in ways that Sainte-Beuve himself deplored) because new forms of distribution offered ways to reach a vaster public that was increasingly literate.

Yet Balzac often tried to create the context of oral storytelling in his written texts. Some of his novels are couched as long narrative letters to a friend or lover that call for a response from the reader. A number of his many novellas and short stories explicitly stage situations where stories are exchanged among members of a given social milieu. For instance, *Another Study of Womankind (Autre Étude de femme)* takes place in the salon of the fictional novelist Félicité des Touches (modeled a bit on George Sand). At the end of a large reception, a small elite group of guests have lingered on for a late supper. The narrator of *Another Study of Womankind*, who won't be identified until late in the tale, notes that such a gathering and the conversation it promotes has become a rare phenomenon in France: it harks back to an ancien régime of greater leisure, when no one was trying to get somewhere, when one could easily pass the night in conversation. So that the oral phenomenon has a quasi-political dimension, as a protest against bourgeois proto-capitalist modern France. Following the Revolution of 1830, which put the bourgeois monarch Louis-Philippe on the throne, time has become the most precious commodity whereas telling stories is a "prodigious prodigality" for those who can talk the night away and sleep in the next morning.[6]

At this afterparty at Félicité des Touches's, "conversation turns toward storytelling." In this situation, "all eyes listen, gestures ask questions, and facial expressions give answers." Never, the narrator tells us, has he been so completely enchanted by the "oral phenomenon." Never has he participated in such a brilliant exchange of stories and comments. As the novella unfolds, within its frame we hear from four principal tellers: Henri de Marsay, Parisian dandy at the summit of his career, now prime minister; the journalist Émile Blondet; General Armand de Montriveau; and at the last, Horace Bianchon himself, the reporter of the whole evening, a celebrated doctor who appears over and over again in *The Human Comedy* as the very model of both dispassionate scientific observation and human sympathy. The tales and reflections are interspersed with comments from the circle of listeners, including a brilliant improvisation on the theme of Napoleon's greatness by the poet Melchior de Canalis. With the exception of Blondet's satiric and analytic description of a new social category, the *"femme comme il faut"*—the "creature of fashion"—they are stories of passion and revenge and social distinction, ending with Bianchon's chilling evocation of a husband burying alive his wife's lover. After that, there is nothing left to say; the guests depart silently. Throughout, it is the reactions to the stories told as much as the tales themselves that hold our interest as indicators of meaning and power. After de Marsay's tale of the infidelity from which he learned to be the cold and self-contained politician, Delphine de Nucingen blurts out: "I pity the second woman" in his series of loves, which provokes an "imperceptible" smile on de Marsay's lips, and our recognition—confirmed by the embarrassed silence of some of the guests—that Delphine herself was that second woman. After Montriveau's horrific tale of a cuckolded husband's vengeance during the retreat of the French Army from Russia, de Marsay makes the comment: "There is nothing more terrible than the revolt of a sheep," a kind of aphoristic summary of what the whole story has been about, yet surely an impoverishment of its meaning.

The evening is summed up by the Baron de Nucingen in his German-Alsatian accent: "Ach! Vhat a bleasure to zit hier tichesting vile you talk!" Food, talk, story, digestion: a traditional context in which to share thoughts and sentiments. In the interstices of telling and listening we grasp that what's more important than any story told is the interactions of teller and listener, the living situation of storytelling. William Labov writes: "In a regular and predictable fashion, certain narratives produce in the audience a profound concentration of attention that creates uninterrupted silence and immobility, an effect that continues long after the ending is reached."[7] That concentration of attention is what Balzac records in *Another Story of Womankind* and elsewhere. Stories matter, he wants to show us: they take a toll, they elicit reactions, they change lives. Storytelling isn't innocent. Balzac often appears to give us a warning like those you see posted at French level crossings: "*Attention. Un train peut en cacher un autre.*" "Watch Out. One train may be hiding another." Other tales may lurk in the interstices of telling and hearing, tales about the relations of teller, told, and listener.

You find simpler versions of what I am talking about in a number of stories by Guy de Maupassant, who became expert in the genre. There is, for example, "A Ruse" ("Une Ruse," 1882), in which the ruse consists precisely in trapping the listener into listening, forcing her to hear a story that she would prefer not to hear, creating a complicity with the incident it recounts that she feels as sullying.[8] In the outer frame of the story, a doctor has just finished his examination of a newlywed woman, suffering from a bit of fatigue and anemia after her first month in a marriage that is a love match (there is a slightly salacious suggestion of too much sex). She tells the doctor she doesn't understand how a wife could be unfaithful to her husband; he responds with a story of such a woman, whose lover dies of a stroke in her bed while her husband is out at his club, but expected home momentarily. The doctor is summoned. Together he and the unfaithful wife dress the corpse, carry it between them down the stairs just as the husband arrives, pretending that the man is not dead but ill and that he and the doctor had been visiting together when the former suffered a momentary seizure. They get the man into the doctor's carriage. Doctor and corpse drive off; the lover's death is then said to take place during the carriage ride, and is so certified. When the doctor has finished his tale, the young woman in his consulting room asks: "Why have you told me this frightful story?" To which he replies: "To offer you my services, should they be needed."

This cynical, mocking—almost sneering—reply that ends the tale reverberates after we have closed the book. What has the doctor done to the young woman? The tale reads as a kind of verbal violation, really a kind of rape, destroying the young woman's faith in marital fidelity, contaminating her mind with ideas it does not want, creating an unwholesome bond between her and her doctor. She has been changed by the story she has unwittingly and unwillingly listened to. She has gained a knowledge of good and evil of which she was innocent. She doesn't want the story, its content, its lesson. But now she cannot get rid of them. They remain with her as a kind of poisonous residue. Maupassant's story is trivial and bleak. But it demonstrates with a kind of fierceness the result of listening, of having to listen to, a story. In the words of T. S. Eliot: "After such knowledge, what forgiveness?" Some things we learn cannot be undone. We are forever changed by them.

At the start of the twentieth century, the English writer Saki (H. H. Munro), perfected a kind of very short story with a final twist that he published with great success in the daily newspaper. "The Open Window" is a very different from Maupassant's tale, but it too turns our attention to the interaction of teller and listener. Framton Nuttel has retreated to the country to soothe his frayed nerves; his sister—who once spent some time in the village—has given him a list of friendly locals. He makes his first call on Mrs. Sappleton. While waiting for her to make her appearance, he is entertained by her "self-possessed" fifteen-year-old niece Vera in a drawing room with a French window open to the lawn. Once Vera (her name suggests she speaks truth) has determined that Nuttel knows nothing about her aunt, she invents. Her aunt's great tragedy, she begins, took place on this very day three years ago. "You may wonder why we keep that window wide open on an October afternoon," she begins—drawing Nuttel's attention to this previously unnoticed feature of the drawing room. The open window then becomes the frame for the story within the story, what we call a framed tale, that Vera tells:

> "Out through that window, three years ago to a day, her husband and her two young brothers went off for their day's shooting. They never came back. In crossing the moor to their favourite snipe-shooting ground they were all three engulfed in a treacherous piece of bog. It had been that dreadful wet summer, you know, and places that were safe in other years gave way suddenly without warning. Their bodies were never recovered. That was the dreadful part of it." Here the child's voice lost its self-possessed note and became falteringly human. "Poor aunt always thinks that they will come back someday, they and the little brown spaniel that was lost with them, and walk in at that window just as they used to do. That is why the window is kept open every evening till it is quite dusk. Poor dear aunt, she has often told me how they went out, her husband with his white waterproof coat over his arm, and Ronnie, her youngest brother, singing 'Bertie, why do you bound?' as he always did to tease her,

because she said it got on her nerves. Do you know, sometimes on still, quiet evenings like this, I almost get a creepy feeling that they will all walk in through that window—"⁹

Vera breaks off "with a little shudder" as Mrs. Sappleton appears.

Mrs. Sappleton rattles on about the weather, the prospects of the hunting season, and other local news; Nuttel talks about his poor health. She says she is waiting for her husband's return with the shooting party, which Nuttel, conditioned by the tragic story he's been told, takes as evidence of obsession and delusion: "all purely horrible." And then Mrs. Sappleton announces: "Here they are at last!...Just in time for tea." Nuttel turns toward Vera. "The child was staring out through the open window with dazed horror in her eyes. In a chill shock of nameless fear Framton swung round in his seat and looked in the same direction," where he sees:

> In the deepening twilight three figures were walking across the lawn towards the window; they all carried guns under their arms, and one of them was additionally burdened with a white coat hung over his shoulders. A tired brown spaniel kept close at their heels. Noiselessly they neared the house, and then a hoarse young voice chanted out of the dusk: "I said, Bertie, why do you bound?"

Nuttel runs from the house as fast as he is able, nearly colliding with a cyclist in the narrow road. It is Mr. Sappleton, returning home, who asks who it was that bolted out, and his wife replies that it was a man who talked of nothing but his illness, and then ran off without apology as if he he'd seen a ghost. As, thanks to Vera's performance, he has.

Now it is Vera who offers an explanation, in the form of an instant fiction, to the baffled Sappletons:

"I expect it was the spaniel," said the niece calmly; "he told me he had a horror of dogs. He was once hunted into a cemetery somewhere on the banks of the Ganges by a pack of pariah dogs, and had to spend the night in a newly dug grave with the creatures snarling and grinning and foaming just above him. Enough to make anyone lose their nerve."

And the story closes with the narrator's comment: "Romance at short notice was her speciality." In fact, romance at short notice was the speciality Saki lived by. But in a larger sense the story is about the power of storytelling. Vera's first story, marked by the generic indicator of tragedy, succeeds in conjuring up ghosts for its listener when the hunters appear, and her second story then allays the ghosts by explaining Nuttel's excessive reaction. Her fictions, for the time the tale lasts, control reality and dictate listener reactions. That "dazed horror" Nuttel reads in her face when the hunters come into sight is a supreme narrative equivocation: Who is responsible for this statement? It is most of all a sign of the power of narrative to dominate reality.

Saki's story is very short and, one might say, deeply frivolous. It offers a good example of how stories can be as much about listeners as tellers, as much about what the story does as what it is. When I discuss stories in the law I will note the importance of creating conviction, which in the law includes both belief in the truth of the story and a legal outcome. Though fictional stories need not decide questions of guilt or innocence, they may raise questions about the responsibilities of storytelling. In *Heart of Darkness*, to take a classic instance, Conrad asks his readers—in the manner that Marlow asks his listeners aboard the *Nellie*—what is to be done with stories that take us into the heart of darkness, whether it be Kurtz's dark adventures or Marlow's lie to Kurtz's Intended. *Heart of Darkness* does not answer these questions but it makes them visible, as it makes visible the darkness that settles at the end of the tale over the Thames: "The offing was barred by a black bank of clouds, and the tranquil waterway leading to the uttermost ends of the earth flowed sombre under an overcast sky—seemed to lead into the heart of an immense darkness."[10]

Many of Balzac's short stories and novellas leave us with similar questions about the force—at times destructive—of storytelling. *Adieu* tells of an attempted cure of a woman who has lost the capacity for speech and reason by means of a creative dramatization that restores her consciousness—but then kills her. *Sarrasine*, another of Balzac's framed tales, ends with an enigmatic evocation of the Marquise de Rochefide, who has been the addressee of the framed story: "And the marquise remained pensive."[11] Many of Balzac's tales result in this kind of "pensiveness," the attitude they aim for and provoke in the listener. Pensiveness indicates the felt force of the story. It leaves the reader, in turn, to ponder its suggested meanings and significance.

Short fiction may be better at dramatizing the reaction of listeners (and readers) than are novels, in which the audience may drop from sight. Though not always. Faulkner's *Absalom, Absalom!*, for instance, stages that dialogue between Quentin and Shreve, in turn listeners and tellers, in their attempt to re-create the Sutpen past, and some of Balzac's full-length novels make the reaction of a listener crucial—perhaps most effectively in *The Lily of the Valley* (*Le Lys dans la vallée*), where Félix de Vandenesse tells the story of his first unhappy love to his new partner, Natalie de Manerville, only to have her turn against him at the very end, claiming that his story reveals the dryness of his heart and his incapacity to experience love again. And there are other narratives that implicate the reader in games of hide-and-seek so that narrative outcomes and evaluations seem to be both more difficult and more important. The relations of both teller and listener, narrator and reader, to what is told lies at the very heart of some challenging fictions.

Take the case of Charlotte Brontë's remarkable *Villette* (1853), in which the orphaned and unsponsored Lucy Snowe leaves England and travels to the fictional Labassecour, much resembling Belgium, where she will become a teacher at Madame Beck's boarding school in Villette. The structure of *Villette* is very different from the framed or embedded narratives I have discussed so far, yet it poses similar questions, in ways that appear both traditional and radical. "Who *are* you, Miss Snowe?" Ginevra Fanshawe will ask, well past the midpoint of the novel, and the reader is constantly engaged with the question.[12] Lucy herself often appears to be asking that question, though at other times she seems largely to understand herself while offering a disguised version to others. But there is a large realm of the unknown in the novel that is only made more opaque in Lucy's narration, which at times hides crucial information from the reader. To read Lucy's story with the requisite attention the reader has to be alertly reactive, like one of Balzac's or Saki's—or Burton's—listeners.

There is, for example, the seemingly trivial yet highly significant story of the watchguard that Lucy makes for M. Paul Emmanuel— head teacher, and someone for whom she has complex feelings—for the fête of his name day, first revealed to the reader in an oblique, somewhat sly manner:

> Well, on the evening in question, we were sitting silent as nuns in a "retreat," the pupils studying, the teachers working. I remember my work; it was a slight matter of fancy, and it rather interested me; it had a purpose; I was not doing it merely to kill time; I meant it when finished as a gift; and the occasion of presentation being near, haste was requisite, and my fingers were busy.

She does not quite tell the reader what she is up to, and this opacity is doubled when she doesn't present the gift during the fête— wounding M. Paul by being the sole member of the community not to give him something. She does so later in the day, however, and the gift is no doubt all the sweeter for the delay, permitting as it does a recognition and reconciliation, in a kind of S/M dynamic typical of this nascent relationship. Yet the game of delay and recognition seems to go on more or less constantly. For instance:

> Now I knew, and had long known, that that hand of M. Emmanuel's was on intimate terms with my desk; that it raised and lowered the lid, ransacked and arranged the contents, almost as familiarly as my own. The fact was not dubious, nor did he wish it to be so; he left signs of each visit palpable and unmistakeable; hitherto, however, I had never caught him in the act.

He leaves her books to read, corrected exercise books, sweetmeats, and the like, and we as readers react that we should have been told this before—that the information revises substantially our understanding of M. Paul's courtship of Lucy. Her revelations of its course to the reader are no more straightforward than her response to M. Paul.

The whole book is a kind of a game of hide-and-seek, or in the more apposite French expression, *un jeu de cache-cache.* Hiding is everywhere, including in the extensive use of French language throughout. When Lucy describes her initial examination by M. Paul at Madame Beck's behest, she says: "I shall go on with this part of my tale as if I had understood all that passed; for though it was then scarce intelligible to me, I heard it translated afterwards." In seeking to explain and justify her account of something she did not understand—because she hadn't yet learned French—Lucy the narrator only creates further opacities. Who could have translated this for her later? M. Paul himself? No one else seems a likely possibility, but having it be M. Paul suggests a zone of opacity we never learn of. It's part of a game of withholding and delayed reporting which might be said to be the mirror image of Madame Beck's spying, the principal method by which she runs her school and one that the novel appears both to criticize and also in its own way to emulate.

During Lucy's first night at Madame Beck's school she becomes aware that Madame Beck herself has entered in her nightgown and undertaken a thorough inspection of Lucy's possessions: searching in the pocket of her dress, counting the money in her purse, inspecting the contents of trunk, desk, and work box, even taking her keys momentarily in order (Lucy surmises) to take wax impressions of them and make duplicates. All this, Lucy concludes, is "very un-English." "'Surveillance,' 'espionage,'—those were her watchwords"—Madame Beck in her silent slippers would "glide ghostlike through the house, watching and spying everywhere, peering through every key-hole, listening behind every door." Later, when Lucy is about to enter the bedroom but is stopped by the sight of Madame Beck once again performing a thorough inspection of her wardrobe, she decides to do nothing—she lets Madame Beck finish her job in peace—and says nothing about it. If she has not joined the surveillance state of Villette, she has at least accepted its existence and perhaps its necessity. Spying and dissimulation are everywhere. Strong Protestant that she is, Lucy claims she has nothing to hide, but little in *Villette* is done or recounted straightforwardly.

During the utter solitude of the long vacation, Lucy falls into despair. She rouses herself at twilight to leave the school, goes to a church in the Old Town, and enters the confessional. Her first words to the priest are: "Mon père, je suis Protestante." ("Father, I am a Protestant.") The ensuing scene lies at the heart of the novel and its narrative complexities. The priest is at a loss to respond: were Lucy Catholic, he says, he would enlist her in the conventual life. In any case, her visit to him represents a sign that she is ready for conversion to the "true faith." He tells her to leave but to return to see him alone at his house the next day. This Lucy knows she must not do:

> The probabilities are that had I visited Numero 10, rue des Mages, at the hour and day appointed, I might just now, instead of writing this heretic narrative, be counting my beads in the cell of a certain Carmelite convent on the Boulevard of Crécy in Villette.

So it is that confession, spoken and heard, central to Catholic dogma and the care of souls for centuries, is set in contrast with the writing of what Lucy calls her "heretic narrative," which I take to mean not only that it insists on her Protestantism and dissent from the Roman Church but that its very form is heretic. While confessional in form—the first-person narrative of a life, and especially an inner life—it does all it can to eschew direct confession, turning instead to a written narrative that, in its avoidances and silences, its refusal to speak directly into the ear presented in the confessional, maintains the right of privacy and dissent. Ginevra's question—"who *are* you?"—produces not an answer but a deferral, an explanatory narrative that rarely speaks directly of Lucy's desire and belief but rather seeks to preserve the freedom from dependence and dogma that allows her to call it "heretic."

After Lucy, leaving the church, faints in the streets of the Old Town as a furious rainstorm breaks out, the novel takes a new turn, with her discovery and repression of her erotic feelings for Graham Bretton. She describes "struggles with the natural character, the strong native bent of the heart," which may seem futile but do at least bring a life "better regulated, more equable, quieter on the surface; and it is on the surface only that the common gaze will fall." And then: "As to what lies below, leave that to God." In other words, no confession except directly to the deity. That's of course largely a Protestant stance—one must speak directly to God, not to the priesthood—and it inflects the whole of Lucy's narrative.

But there is no assurance that the outer world will be transparent to Lucy's sensitive consciousness. The hallucinatory climactic scene at the public fête in the park, which Lucy comes to in an exalted state since she's been drugged by Madame Beck—who wants M. Paul for herself—leads to revelations that actually create more errors of perception. These will be corrected only later, when M. Paul leads her to the house in the Faubourg Clotilde—which is to be the new school that Lucy will direct —and proposes marriage. But the novel does not end on this kind of happy resolution. M. Paul must go to Guadeloupe on a voyage lasting three years. "And now the three years are past: M. Emmanuel's return is fixed." There is no temporal anchor to that "now": is it the time of Lucy's narrating? Then comes her report of the great seven-day storm on the Atlantic that presumably destroys the ship on which M. Paul sails as well as so many others. But the outcome is left to the reader's imagination and choice in a rhetorical flourish in which Lucy appears to abandon her very position as narrator of her story, to give up the knowledge of its outcome that she should possess.

As a narrator, Lucy not only eludes us but at times positively deceives us. Yet such elusiveness may be what is needed for Lucy to avoid limiting definitions—"the spinster," for instance—that would reduce and pin down her ambiguities and evasions. It is the precondition of her freedom. I see *Villette* as a precursor of novels that refuse to offer an authoritative telling—such as those of Proust and Faulkner. The elusive, unstable narrating *I* of *Villette* makes uncertainty and instability the very principle of story and storytelling, and of self-knowledge. Perhaps the nescience I associated with James's *The Beast in the Jungle* and Lafayette's *The Princess of Clèves* would be the appropriate term: the realm of the unknown, and even never knowable, is what drives the quest for narrative knowledge. Ginevra's "Who *are* you, Miss Snowe?" never receives an adequate answer, surely because there is no true answer to such a question. Character is not so stable. And when it is a matter of Lucy's attempting to know and say what she is, only new questions can result. Teller and tale circle round one another to a necessarily uncertain outcome. But that uncertainty may appear more honest, more true to our own experience, than the neat outcomes of other novels.

Villette points in this manner to the numerous novels that resist the traditional dependence on plot and the end-oriented structure of narrative meaning, which claim something like the superior authenticity of the apparently unedited story. The French "new novel" of the 1950s and '60s, and current "autofiction," for instance, reject standard novelistic structure and devices as untrue to the flux of existence. Yet the resistance to an orderly sense of form that we find in Charlotte Brontë or in such contemporary novelists as Rachel Cusk or Sheila Heti actually seems to me no less present throughout the tradition of the novel, starting with *Don Quixote* and passing through Dickens and Flaubert and Proust into the present era. There is a continual conflict of form and the formless. The novel struggles to create form in the transitory and chaotic passage of human life, attempting to impose a readable structure on experience in time, admitting its defeat.

Walter Benjamin's essay "The Storyteller" provides further perspective on the question I began with: how the written text engages with oral storytelling, as well as the challenges of telling that I described in *Villette*. "The Storyteller" opposes the oral tale to the printed novel. The tale comes to life in the milieu of work and travel and trade: it is an oral transaction in the workshop or a traveler's story of adventure upon returning home. Above all, it involves one person transmitting experience of life to another, in a vital exchange. The personality of the storyteller clings to the story "the way the traces of the potter's hand cling to a clay bowl," Benjamin writes.[13] Stories are compact, they have a "chaste brevity" that precludes explanation. They unfold within the rhythms of life and work. The tale offers human counsel; it transmits what Benjamin calls, simply, wisdom.

But storytelling is dying out, and with it so is the art of listening as practiced in a community of listeners—like that dramatized in Balzac's *Another Study of Womankind*—gathered around the storyteller. And there is even the threat of losing the very communicability of experience: we no longer know how to share our experiences, a condition Benjamin takes to be caused and symbolized by the shock of the Great War and its sequels:

> A generation that had gone to school in horse-drawn streetcars found itself under open sky in a landscape in which only the clouds were unchanged and below them, in a force field crossed by devastating currents and explosions, stood the tiny, fragile human body.

Benjamin quotes the opinion of Nikolai Leskov (the ostensible subject of his essay) that storytelling is not high art but a craft—"*ein Handwerk*"—and this leads him to reflect on Paul Valéry's meditations on Marie Monnier's elaborate embroidery, the product of infinite patience, the unhurried acquisition of perfection. "The era is past when time did not matter," writes Valéry. "Today no one cultivates what cannot be created quickly." And then, in one of Benjamin's sleight-of-hand transitions, this loss of patient handwork is comparable to the fading of the "idea of eternity," which in turn suggests that the "idea of death has lost persuasiveness and immediacy in the collective consciousness." Death has ceased to be public, and in the process it has lost its authority, yet that is the authority that "lies at the very source of the story."

And now Benjamin can make what may be the central pronouncement of his essay: "Death is the sanction of everything the storyteller can relate. It is death that has lent him his authority." This authority of death sets up the contrast to the novel, which he sees, in the extraordinary phrase from Georg Lukács's *Theory of the Novel*, as the "form of transcendental homelessness." Lukács sets the novel in contrast to the epic, where meaning inhabits the life of the hero. Meaning is immanent to life. The novel is another matter. There, "meaning is separated from life, and hence the essential from the temporal: we might almost say that the entire inner action of the novel is nothing but a struggle against the power of time." Lukács in fact underlines the essential role of temporality in the novel. Those novels that best define the genre for us tend to be long—from Richardson's *Clarissa* through Dickens's and Balzac's and Brontë's and Dostoevsky's and George Eliot's huge productions, and on to Henry James and Proust—because their meanings must be played out over passing time: people age, make mistakes, regret decisions, choose new partners, perhaps learn something about life. This, for Lukács, incidentally makes Flaubert's *Sentimental Education* (*L'Education sentimentale*) the novel of novels, one in which the failure to wrest meaning from the struggle with time leads, at the end, to the compensation of telling stories about that failure, as the book's protagonist Frédéric and his friend Deslauriers meet to "exhume" their youth, the only pleasure left to them. "Only in the novel," Lukács claims, "does memory occur as a creative force affecting the object and transforming it."

Now, Benjamin sees Lukács as illuminating a fundamental distinction between story and novel. In the first, we have "the moral of the story"; in the novel, the question is rather the "meaning of life." The listener to the story is in the company of the storyteller, but the reader of the novel is "solitary, more so than any other reader." He appropriates the novel, "devours the book's contents as fire consumes logs in the fireplace." What readers look for in the novel is closed to them in their own lives: the knowledge of death that they cannot have in life and which alone confers meaning on life. It is with the end of a life that its meaning becomes apparent. In the death of the fictional character, Benjamin claims: "The flame that consumes this stranger's fate warms us as our own fates cannot. What draws the reader to a novel is the hope of warming his shivering life at the flame of a life he reads about."

Novels depend on their endings in a way that contrasts with the living communication of wisdom in the tale. Novels belong to a time—in broad strokes, our modernity—where that commonality between teller and listener has been shattered. In its place, novels bring a simulacrum of sociality in listening to a story told to the solitary individual. In illuminating the meaning of life through the significant death, the novel offers its different form of wisdom. The novelistic tradition often makes much of the deathbed, from Clarissa Harlowe's edifying end—"O death! Where is thy sting?" she exclaims—to Old Goriot's final rants about his daughters' betrayals and the collapse of family and society in Balzac's *Père Goriot*, on to Milly Theale's final absolution of Merton Densher's deception of her in James's *The Wings of the Dove*. These moments of transition from life to death, often from one generation to another, offer the transmission of a kind of wisdom, a final summing-up on life.

A very old legal doctrine of "dying declarations," captured in the Latin phrase *nemo moriturus praesumitur mentire* (a dying person is not presumed to lie) still survives in the law today.[14] It dominates a doleful literary genre that came to the fore in the late seventeenth century, the so-called "Newgate Biography": confessional narratives taken by the Ordinary (the chaplain) of Newgate Prison from those about to hang at the Tyburn gallows, then written down and published as chapbooks. These cost sixpence and sold quite well, adding a handsome supplement—as much as £200—to the Ordinary's ecclesiastical stipend. The genre flourished for about a century, from 1676 to 1772, and offered accounts of some 2,500 hangings, presented with a title page along the lines of: "The Ordinary of Newgate's / Account of the / Behaviour, Confessions, and Dying Words / of the six Malefactors/Who were executed at Tyburn / on Monday the 11th of November, 1751 / Being the First Execution in the Mayoralty / of the / Rt. Honorable Thomas Winterbottom, Esq. / Lord-Mayor of London." These sensational and moralistic tales recount ordinary lives gradually slipping into crime, as many an idle apprentice, for instance, will end up robbing his master or setting his house afire. The accounts tend to take their subjects from the moment of conviction at the Old Bailey to the moment of execution, scrutinizing especially their expressions of remorse and religious faith, and showing particular attention to professions of belief at the very last. They are presented sometimes as first-person accounts, or else in indirect summary narration ("He says that next . . ."). But of course they are "as told to"—to this professional biographer, who is also a representative of the Church of England.[15] They may resemble the confessions produced in present-day custodial interrogations, where the words of the suspect-perpetrator are lent to him or her by the police. Even when narrated in the first person they might be characterized as hearsay. Their popularity no doubt had much to do with the heinous crimes they recounted—they at times foreshadow the Gothic tales and the penny dreadfuls of the Victorians—all the while promoting pious thoughts.[16] Above all, they stress finality: how one behaves, what one confesses, what one speaks in his or her dying words. They evince a continuing fascination with the threshold moment of passage from life to death, and with the question of what possible illumination may emanate from that ultimate instant.

In his claim that death is the "sanction" of narrative, Benjamin reaches back to this tradition that believes the moment of death to be a moment of truth telling. At the same time, he subscribes to a view that Proust expounds: that reading a narrative is the only *meaningful* experience we can have of life. Telling trumps living, as in the final scene of Flaubert's *Sentimental Education.* Memory has become transformative. Yet that is a sad wisdom, which may make us want to recover the live communicative situation of storytelling. There is in Benjamin, here as elsewhere, a sophisticated nostalgia that holds in balance loss and the insight it provides. "The art of storytelling is coming to an end because the epic side of truth, that is, wisdom, is dying out," he writes. But then he adds: "This phenomenon is far from new. Nothing would be more foolish than to consider it merely a 'symptom of decline' much less a 'modern' symptom. It is, rather, a side effect of historical secular forces of productivity that have gradually eliminated the storyteller from the realm of living speech and at the same time have made a new beauty visible in what has disappeared." In Balzac's stories of storytelling—and those of other nineteenth-century writers—we observe the power of storytelling in action while also feeling the dialectical nostalgia brought into being by the "historical secular forces of productivity."

Benjamin understands that orality can now be preserved only through literacy. He surely knows that Leskov himself was an example of a later and sophisticated simulation of orality. His preference for the oral tale over the novel is at the same time sincere and strategic. It enables him, as he puts it, to see the beauty in what is vanishing and to suggest, along with Lukács, why the novel has become the modern genre that has eclipsed, maybe devoured, all others. Benjamin offers an earlier version of his polemic on the reading of novels in a 1930 article on Döblin's *Berlin Alexanderplatz*: the novelist, he says, "is the truly solitary, silent individual. . . . The birthplace of the novel is the individual in his solitude who is no longer able to speak about his most important concerns in an exemplary way, who has no one to counsel him and has no counsel to offer." The novel, he claims, has attained an "outrageous proportion" in our reading.

But such statements imply a recognition that there is no turning back from the role that novels have come to play in our self-understandings and our ways of deciphering other people within modernity. There is no way out from the novel, and the indebtedness of "The Storyteller" to Lukács's *Theory of the Novel* shows clearly enough that whatever nostalgia Benjamin harbors for the epic and the oral exists within the context of the written. So it is that he praises Arnold Bennett's *The Old Wives' Tale* on the twenty-fifth anniversary of its publication, in 1933: "Of all the gifts [the novel] offers, this is the most certain: the end. . . . The novel is not important because it portrays the fate of a stranger for us, but because the flame that consumes that stranger's fate warms us as our own fates cannot. What draws the reader to the novel again and again is its mysterious ability to warm a shivering life with death." There we are again: in the forlornness of our modern condition, deprived of "counsel," it is the novel that brings us warmth through its capacity to make us understand the end.

Storytelling risks degradation by its promiscuous overuse in public life. "Story," as I noted in chapter 1, has entered the orbit of political cant and corporate branding. The media proclaims story everywhere, as if that were the only form of understanding left in our civilization. This saturation of our culture by the mindless promotion of story argues the need for Benjamin's rich and acid analysis of culture by way of its literary exemplars, themselves largely dissenters from cultural consensus. Critical attention to the way stories are told and the way they work on us, their listeners, is ever more crucial, in politics, in law, in narratives of "who we are," as a nation as well as individuals. Failure to understand the rhetoric of narrative and its persuasive effects has consequences for the polity itself. Benjamin's analysis of the dying arts of telling and listening to stories is at once an affirmation that other forms—and all forms—of narrative need to be analytically engaged because they are crucial to our self-understandings. He concludes his essay: "The storyteller is the figure in which the righteous man encounters himself." A vatic statement. But the essay as a whole has convinced us equally that beyond righteousness in any simple sense the novel at its most powerful offers us our best understandings of what it means to live, to have lived, to construct a life.

I have spent these pages on Benjamin because, for all the twists and slippages in his argument, he poses better than most the stakes of narrative, be it in tale or novel. Narrative may be the best discursive and analytic tool that we have for transmitting what we know about life, and for constructing a life in time as something that has shape and meaning—to a point. Lucy Snowe's self-narrative is a particularly telling case of someone trying to rescue the meaning of a self that others ignore or denigrate, in a "heretic narrative" that needs hiding and indirection as well as self-assertion if she is to maintain her freedom from simplifying definitions. Balzac's and Saki's scenes of narrative exchange suggest that we need narrative to make experience transmissible. Like the stories told and retold in the law, these examples argue that finding and telling the story that carries conviction is a nontrivial endeavor. Which in turn argues that our analytic tools for studying narrative are important.

4. The Allure of Imaginary Beings

WHY DO WE INVEST so much time and emotional energy in our relationships with imaginary beings? Why are the aspirations, the errors, the inner turmoil and erotic daydreams of Emma Woodhouse and Emma Bovary so important to us? We know when we open the novels in which they figure that the persons we are going to meet aren't "real," yet that makes us no less eager to meet them, no less highly invested in how we feel about them, how we admire and criticize them, how we anticipate their emotional highs and lows, how we fear for their failures and hope for their successes. Reading Richardson's *Clarissa* and *Pamela*, Denis Diderot shows himself to be ideally engaged: "How many times have I not caught myself, like children taken to the theater for the first time, crying aloud: *Don't believe him, he is deceiving you. . . . If you go there, you will be lost.* My soul was held in constant agitation."[1] Diderot recognizes that this is an extreme case of a reader's identification with fictional characters and their situations. Yet he models what in more muted and attenuated form must be the reaction of all readers who find themselves "caught up" (as we put it) in the reading of a novel. Those unreal people and their dilemmas are deeply important to us. The psychologist Paul Harris confirms what we already know: fictions arouse emotions even when recognized to be fictional.[2] Invented persons are vehicles of emotion that we seem to need. Like the imaginary mothers and fathers and siblings of children's play, the imagined persons of novels are freighted with desire, admiration, fear.

And yet we know all along that these beings really exist only in writing. There was a time when avant-garde criticism dismissed literary characters as a misguided nineteenth-century illusion that we could do without. And in teaching novels I always urged my students to step back from that illusion, to examine how it is constructed in language. Yet even when we detach ourselves from the illusion and look at character as a linguistic construction, we discover its appeal and necessity. And recently criticism has seen a revival of attention to character, though with much uncertainty as to how to talk about it.[3] It's not easy to talk about. One way into discussion might be by means of what happens when our favorite literary characters are impersonated in film and television adaptations, given a visual, corporeal literalization. We all have had the experience of reacting: That's not it. That's not how I imagined Elizabeth Bennet or Jay Gatsby when reading the novels in which they figure. Or conversely, the experience of finding that a film has captured our imagined version of a character so well that it takes over the image that we afterwards carry of that person. But such perfect incarnations are uncommon. More often than not, visual versions bring a certain dissonance, if not a sense of downright betrayal. For instance, I have never seen an adaptation of *Madame Bovary* that I found at all satisfactory: Emma Bovary may be very difficult to literalize because she is herself a creature of daydream, fantasy, the wish to be other and elsewhere. Her virtue for us as readers lies partly in her noncoherence as a flesh and blood creature. Emma creates issues in understanding, sympathy, and judgment rather than solving them. Our preference for the verbal construct over the image makes us want to understand better the workings of imagination.

Our sense of fictional character is a mental and emotional construct; it has a visual component but remains in the realm of play and daydream, a creative fantasy that is not necessarily realized by the attempt to embody it in the more literal medium of film. Proust offers a subtle and helpful understanding of how character in fiction works.[4] There is a moment in *In Search of Lost Time* when the young Marcel is reading a novel in the garden gazebo, and his absorption in the novel is described as creating a kind of bright, diaphanous screen between him as reader and external world, which is erased and subsumed into the fictional world that comes to seem more real. The invention of the fictional character, says Proust, enables us to experience life through other eyes. This eventually will lead—hundreds of pages later—to a soaring flight of fancy:

> The only true voyage, the only bath in the Fountain of Youth, would be not to visit strange lands but to possess other eyes, to see the universe through the eyes of another, of a hundred others, to see the hundred universes that each of them sees, that each of them is; and this we can do with an Elstir, with a Vinteuil; with men like these we do really fly from star to star.[5]

Over the course of Proust's novel, the creations of his fictional painter Elstir and his fictional composer Vinteuil come to figure precisely the promise of other optics on the world, a simulation of what it would mean to inhabit another being.

Returning to the scene of reading in the garden in *Swann's Way*—

Marcel has been sent to read outside since his grandmother has pronounced the weather too fine to remain indoors—we find Proust's most focused statement on character in the novel. It is true, the narrator tells us, that the characters in the book are not what the literal-minded maid Françoise would call "real."

> But all the feelings we are made to experience by the joy or the misfortune of a real person are produced in us only through the intermediary of an image of that joy or that misfortune; the ingeniousness of the first novelist consisted in understanding that in the apparatus of our emotions, the image being the only essential element, the simplification that would consist in purely and simply abolishing real people would be a decisive improvement. A real human being, however profoundly we sympathize with him, is in large part perceived by our senses, that is to say, remains opaque to us, presents a dead weight which our sensibility cannot lift. . . . The novelist's happy discovery was to have the idea of replacing these parts [of real persons], impenetrable to the soul, by an equal quantity of immaterial parts, that is to say, parts which our soul can assimilate. What does it matter thenceforth if the actions, and the emotions, of this new order of creatures seem to us true, since we have made them ours, since it is within us that they occur, that they hold within their control, as we feverishly turn the pages of the book, the rapidity of our breathing and the intensity of our gaze.[6]

To be inhabited in this manner by the fictional is to be troubled as by a dream, but it's more lucid than a dream, and it allows us to discover in the space of a couple of hours what it would take us years to learn in life—or that we might not learn at all since the profound changes in life are hidden from us by the slowness of their process. The heart changes in life; that is our worst sorrow; but we know this change only in reading.

For Proust, life can be understood only in fiction. Living is blind. Fiction alone provides a recovery of meaning from passing time, and fictional beings are crucial to the project because their eyes allow us to see the meanings of temporal change. Proust prefigures Benjamin's claim that we seek in fiction knowledge of the meaning of death that is foreclosed to us in our own lives, but for Proust it is above all imagined characters that make this possible. The critic Catherine Gallagher similarly argues that it is the very fictionality of novelistic characters that allows them to represent the real for us.[7] It's in fact "representation" that matters: the heightened legibility of the fictional person, which allows us to know things that in reality we can't know. By suppressing "real people," Proust's imagined "first novelist" extends our minds and emotions, enabling us to see the world around us in radically other ways. Once we see through other eyes, we are transformed. It's our everyday selves that become merely virtual.

Optics are crucial throughout the *Recherche*. The eyes of others are an allure, and a frustration. There is, for instance, the moment Marcel first sees Albertine, as yet a stranger to him. She appears with her bicycle amidst the "*petite bande*" of girlfriends on the seafront of the Norman town of Balbec. He is seized by her appearance and zeroes in on her eyes:

If we thought that the eyes of such a girl are only shining chips of mica, we wouldn't be avid to know her life and to join it to our own. But we sense that what shines in this reflective disk is not only due to its material composition; that these are, unbeknownst to us, the black shadows of the thoughts that this being forms, relative to the people and things it meets—turf of the racetracks, sand of the paths where, pedaling through fields and wood, this little Peri, more seductive for me than that of the Persian paradise, would have led me—the shadows too of the house where she will return home, the projects that she is forming or that others have formed for her; and especially that it is she, with her desires, her sympathies, her repulsions, her obscure and unceasing will. I knew that I would not possess this young cyclist unless I possessed also what was in her eyes.[8]

It is our knowledge that a consciousness is lodged behind those chips of mica, that someone is looking out at us through them, that is the source of our longing and our torture. We want to be able to take up our dwelling behind those eyes, to know intimately everything that they know in the course of a day and a night. Here begins the painful and impossible desire to make another's life one's own, the scenario that will play out over a thousand or so pages and lead to Marcel sequestering Albertine, like a prisoner, in his Parisian apartment—until she escapes, in a flight that ends in her death. But Marcel's encounter with Albertine speaks not only of the impossibility of possessing another person, it also lays the groundwork for recognition that it is only through the art of the painter, the composer—and the novelist—that we can enter behind the eyes of another.

Proust's understanding of the novel as the place of imagined lives that enable us to dis-place ourselves from our own lives may look like a more advanced version of a traditional apologia for the novel as extending our sympathies, one that easily flips into the critique of the novel: since it displaces us from our normal place of moral residence, it can make us lose our moral compass, espouse unbridled erotic experiences and long for forbidden emotions. It's the source of the long suspicion of the novel on the part of churchmen and moralists, given perhaps its most sophisticated discussion by Jean-Jacques Rousseau, who both castigates the fictional simulation and stimulation of the emotions, and makes the French eighteenth century's most celebrated use of them in his one novel, *The New Heloise* (*Julie; ou La nouvelle Héloïse*), which begins with the epigraph: "Theatre is necessary in large cities, and novels for corrupt populations. I have looked at the manners of my time, and published these letters. If only I had lived in a time when I should have thrown them in the fire!"[9] That is to say, once emotions have become the stuff of feigning, of theater, of cultivation, then one needs to employ the very genre, the novel, in which internalizing the feigned emotions of another can lead you through corruption to something else. The novel is given a nearly theological role: it is the vehicle that makes the fall redeemable. It is the place of the *felix culpa*.

In Proust's *Recherche*, this fall into knowledge occurs most strikingly at the outset of *Sodom and Gomorrah*, where Marcel discovers what he calls sexual "inversion"—homosexuality—in a number of important figures of his world, which profoundly changes his understanding of society as well as sexuality. Proust's large claim about the value of fictions, as I understand it, lies in the morality that may be said to inhere in the extension of a single life and consciousness into multiple and diverse others. The more these others may "invert" us the better. The more they unsettle our preconceptions and self-satisfactions the better. This to Proust represents the ethics of fictionality. The reader's relation to fictional characters is less a matter of identification, as we were once, lazily, taught to think, than what Proust calls metempsychosis, reincarnation in another's alien body. And it is a willed metempsychosis, something we go in search of whenever we open a novel, in an act of what Henry James called immersion. But again, what this might mean needs further scrutiny if we are to understand the cognitive and ethical value of fictional beings.

Proust's concern with optics—with seeing the world through the eyes of another, of many others—leads him in the late pages of *Time Regained* (*Le Temps retrouvé*) to state: "In reality, each reader is when he reads the very reader of himself. The work of the writer is only a kind of optical instrument that he offers the reader in order to allow him to discern what, without this book, he might not have seen in himself."[10] Represented persons give us an understanding of life, and of ourselves, that real persons cannot. Why is that? In daily life what Proust calls "habit" fills us with a lazy blindness; the novel as optical instrument alone restores vision. Recent work on literature and cognitive neuroscience that stresses "theory of mind" arrives at a like understanding. The novel is seen to call on us, and teach us, to understand what is going on in the minds of others, on multiple levels—as in Edgar Allan Poe's "The Purloined Letter," where Auguste Dupin begins the work of detection by imagining the "robber's knowledge of the loser's knowledge of the robber." This can be extended to further levels: we can attempt to understand how some other person might have knowledge of another's knowledge but consider that the other's knowledge of her knowledge might alter the other's thinking about that knowledge, and so on. Neuroscientists have noted that we are capable of going up at least four levels.[11] I suspect in Henry James it may be more. In *The Wings of the Dove*, for instance, characters can deduce the existence of invisible persons by their occult influence on the visible ones, in the manner that astronomers have deduced the existence of invisible bodies from their gravitational effect on the orbits of the visible ones. And in James's most audacious experiment, *The Sacred Fount*, the whole story is extrapolated from the narrator's private vision of the vampiric interactions among his fellow houseguests.

Proust has only increased in popularity over time, I think because his claims for the cognitive and ethical value of fictions are very much of our moment. We may today be ready to restore the imagination to the place of honor it occupied for Coleridge and other Romantics, though we have come no closer to understanding how it works. Since such as Roland Barthes and Michel Foucault taught us to see selves as coded structures produced by culture and society, paradoxically this has allowed us to relax somewhat about the loss of self involved in the reading of fictions. If, in the Rousseauian argument, we lose our moral compass when we assimilate fictional lives to our own and start to view the world through other eyes, so much the better, we may decide. We may want to go so far as the claim advanced by Lynn Hunt, in her *Inventing Human Rights*, that our imaginative investment in other selves lies at the origin of our capacity to understand others as having irreducible rights that cannot be violated: precisely our understanding of what is human.[12] And this understanding is now leading many to think about the claims of nonhuman species in relation to us.

Long before Proust, Adam Smith argued in his *Theory of Moral Sentiments* that the imagination gives us the power of sympathetic or empathetic identification. His famous passage on torture (which should be required reading in the CIA):

Though our brother is upon the rack, as long as we ourselves are at our ease, our senses never will inform us of what he suffers.... By the imagination we place ourselves in his situation, we conceive ourselves enduring all the same torments, we enter as it were into his body, and become in some measure the same person with him, and thence form some idea of his sensations, and even feel something which, though weaker in degree, is not altogether unlike them. His agonies, when they are thus brought home to ourselves, when we have thus adopted and made them our own, begin at last to affect us, and we then tremble and shudder at the thought of what he feels.[13]

Like Proust, Smith is alert to the movement *between* self and other that the imagination permits. He does not take Proust's further step: that using a fictional person instead of "our brother" makes espousing his body and mind more complete, a substitution more than a simulation, and thus, paradoxically, a fuller realization of another kind of being in the world.

That is a potent argument in favor of fictions, a strong justification of our modern choice of the novel to represent everything we think we want to know, from past history to future dystopia as well as countless scenes of contemporary life. But we need also to recall what Proust tells us about the price paid for novelistic representation during the final pages of *Time Regained*—pages of a triumphant joy at his vocation at last discovered, but with a dark undercurrent that we should not neglect. The discovery of his vocation means, for Marcel, the renunciation of those he has loved, destined to become imaginary figures in the fiction. Persons are erased by the novelist. Marcel calls a novel a "vast cemetery where on most of the gravestones one can no longer read the names that have been effaced."[14] Cognition is incorporate with extinction and destruction: people must die for the novel to live. The death of the novelist, too, is part of the life of the fiction: he is like Scheherazade, who tells stories to ward off death. The world of fictional characters has no place for the "real" and the "living." The power of novels to illuminate our lives depends on the alchemy that creates fictional beings as vessels of our consciousness. The novel, the instrument for seeing the world through the eyes of others, becomes in *Time Regained* an instrument for reading oneself with a renewed vision, turning, so to speak, the eyes of all those others on ourselves through the instrumentality of the novel.

What does this tell us about our quest to understand fictional characters and how we use them? I'm not sure I can offer anything definitive here, but I would suggest that our love of fictional characters and our willingness to spend time with them and to let them seep into our everyday "real" lives, and also our reluctance to let go of them once our reading of the fiction is over, our continuing conversation about them, maybe with them, is largely as Proust describes it: a wish to travel from star to star through the vision provided by new sets of eyes, by new optical instruments. This is in the best of cases, in the novels we value most, not a passive or escapist process but one that has a cognitive and critical function. Character in the novel gives us, in the old yet still fresh words of Matthew Arnold, a "criticism of life."

The cognitive value of the fictional person—that person as cognitive instrument—both affirms our traditional sense of the "real life" of literary characters and paradoxically returns those characters to our own minds, now enlarged by their encounter with imagined persons. The literary character is both alive and no one, the image used by our consciousness. Proust's notion of character I think points toward that of his avid reader, Samuel Beckett: character as the Unnameable, *L'Innommable.* Character belongs to mind, ultimately the reader's, a consciousness lodged somewhere between Scheherazade's and the sultan's, in what Jacques Rancière calls the "suspensive space" of reading in which one is everyone and no one.[15] It is not, for me, a matter of "incarnation," which seems to underlie Rancière's discussion of flesh and word. Our embodiment by way of the characters whose lives we read about is itself fictional, provisional, a trying-on of costumes, manners, sensations, eyeglasses—including telescopes and microscopes—that is protean in its mobility. That we can talk about Dorothea Brooke or Eugène de Rastignac beyond the boundaries of the pages we have read is testimony not so much to our wish that we could invite them to dinner with us as to our need to reimagine our own existences through their eyes. As Freud said, much too simplistically but with much truth, fiction is all about "His Majesty, the ego." Freud also says in his essay *The Ego and the Id* that the "character of the ego is a precipitate of abandoned object-cathexes and that it contains the history of those object choices."[16] I translate this to mean that the ego is built from those objects, meaning largely persons, which have been invested with desire over time and which, even when abandoned, contribute to the structuring of the ego. And I think we can include in those "abandoned object-cathexes" (that is, the places to which libido was once attached) fictional persons as well as real ones. The ego learns its own shape by trying on others. The more cognitively challenging the process, the better. That's why we need the novel.

I have mentioned the Romantic preoccupation with the imagination, and what I have been trying to discern in our understanding and use of fictional characters reminds me of John Keats's notion of "negative capability": "that is when a man is capable of being in uncertainties, Mysteries, doubts, without any irritable reaching after fact & reason." Keats develops this thought in his letter to Richard Woodhouse of 1818:

> As to the poetical Character itself (I mean that sort of which, if I am any thing, I am a Member; that sort distinguished from the word-sworthian or egotistical sublime; which is a thing per se and stands alone) it is not itself—it has no self—it is every thing and nothing— It has no character—it enjoys light and shade; it lives in gusto, be it foul or fair, high or low, rich or poor, mean or elevated—It has as much delight in conceiving an Iago as an Imogen. What shocks the virtuous philosopher, delights the camelion Poet. It does no harm from its relish of the dark side of things any more than from its taste for the bright one; because they both end in speculation. A Poet is the most unpoetical of any thing in existence; because he has no Identity—he is continually in for—and filling some other Body.[17]

Readers, like poets and novelists, are also chameleon poets, taking joy in Iago as well as Imogen, provisionally giving up personal identity in order to be in and filling some other body: not incarnation, I think, so much as Proust's metempsychosis, a shape-shifting.

Proust's conception of "character" and the reader's response to it bears comparison to Virginia Woolf's. Woolf doesn't abandon the concept of literary character, but she works to smudge its clear outlines, to suggest that the person is far more fluid and changeable and hard to pin down than earlier novelists had indicated. In her famous essay "Mr. Bennett and Mrs. Brown" (also known as "Character in Fiction"), she offers her forceful riposte to the Edwardian novelist Arnold Bennett, who had, in his review of her *Jacob's Room*, accused her of creating characters that would not endure. Woolf replies: "[Mr. Bennett] says that it is only if the characters are real that the novel has any chance of surviving. Otherwise, die it must. But, I ask myself, what is reality? And who are the judges of reality?" She claims, in the phrase most often quoted from the essay: "On or about December 1910 human character changed." Which may be to say, at the least, that representations of human character changed as modernist understandings of motivation and the composition of the person changed, under the impulsion of Freud as of many another thinker and artist. Woolf doesn't wish to abolish character. What she does (in the manner of Proust, with James clearly a precursor) is to dissolve its hard outlines, its nature as a fully upholstered Victorian being, in favor of something that seeks to change our optics.

"Mr. Bennett and Mrs. Brown" takes issue with Bennett's idea of character by imagining a woman, Mrs. Brown, who has sat down opposite her in a railway carriage. Bennett would describe her by way of externals: where she is from, what kind of house she lives in, its furnishings, her income, her father's profession, what her mother died of. And so on. [18]

"'Describe cancer. Describe calico. Describe—'" But I cried, "Stop! Stop!" And I regret to say that I threw that ugly, that clumsy, that incongruous tool out of the window, for I knew that if I began describing the cancer and the calico, my Mrs. Brown, that vision to which I clung though I know no way of imparting it to you, would have been dulled and tarnished for ever."

Bennett's kind of description descends from Dickens and Balzac and Eliot and indeed most nineteenth-century novelists. Woolf claims that the notion one can get at character this way gets everything backwards. It is fine to endow Mrs. Brown with whatever traits you want, but it is most important to understand that she is an optics on the world. She is our instrument for seeing. She makes our minds and imaginations work trying to understand her view of the world, and that can never be got at by externalities.

This leads me to another great experimental investigator of fictional character, Henry James, who in his novella *The Beast in the Jungle* presents a perverse and sinister version of the concerns I have attributed to Proust. I am thinking of the moment in the novella—eminently a tale of character and nothingness—when John Marcher's woman companion (but no more than that) May Bartram manages to peer through the mask of Marcher's persona. Marcher's life, lived in expectation of the spring of the "beast," of something important and unexpected, becomes a long exercise in egotistical self-absorption, neglecting the love that May offers him, doing essentially nothing while he awaits the moment that never comes. May is the one who will come to see the nothingness of his life. Marcher's social behavior is described as a "long act of dissimulation." The following lines are more radical still:

> What it had come to was that he wore a mask painted with the social simper, out of the eye-holes of which there looked eyes of an expression not in the least matching the other features. This the stupid world, even after years, had never more than half-discovered. It was only May Bartram who had, and she achieved, by an art indescribable, the feat of at once—or perhaps it was only alternately—meeting

the eyes from in front and mingling her own vision, as from over his shoulder, with their peep through the apertures.[19]

May Bartram appears as the perfect reader of fiction, whose "art indescribable" both espouses Marcher's optics on the world, from behind his mask, and confronts it from outside him. She discovers truth—and later on can only plead that the truth never come out.

James presents a moralized—one might say, an American—view of the fictional mask. More than any other novelist I know, he makes us think of the relations of the two ways in which we most often talk of "character": the fictional person and the moral being. These are distinct uses of the word and the concept, yet in our reading they frequently intersect: we may judge fictional characters in terms of their moral being. Yet the morality play in *The Beast in the Jungle* is itself complex: if it is about an ethical failure of empathy, a failure on Marcher's part to put himself in the place of May, it is more radically about the fearful possibility that "character" is itself nothingness, merely an assumed fiction, a mask, part of a bogus metaphysics. But for neither Proust nor James is this nothingness thinkable except in human terms, as consequences of what human actors do, and fail to do. When Marcher at the end reaches his illumination—sparked by the stricken face of another mortal who has lost the woman he loved—it is very much about a person, about May Bartram and his failure to respond to her love. The "sounded void of his life," as it is designated in the next to last paragraph of the tale, is both an abyss of unknowing and a personal experience of loss. Unknowing in *The Beast in the Jungle* is lived as a human, personal experience; it comes as a discovery that Marcher must at the last make, so that the melodramatic climax of the story represents the knowledge of his lifelong nescience as that very beast: "This horror of waking—this was knowledge, knowledge under the breath of which the very tears in his eyes seemed to freeze.... He saw the Jungle of his life and saw the lurking Beast; then, while he looked, perceived it, as by a stir of the air, rise, huge and hideous, for the leap that was to settle him. His eyes darkened—it was close; and, instinctively turning, in his hallucination, to avoid it, he flung himself, face down, on the tomb."

Earlier in the story, May, who already has begun to see the outcome, tells Marcher that he can only go on as he is:

> It was into this going on as he was that they relapsed, and really for so long a time that the day inevitably came for a further sounding of their depths. These depths, constantly bridged over by a structure firm enough in spite of its lightness and of its occasional oscillation in the somewhat vertiginous air, invited on occasion, in the interest of their nerves, a dropping of the plummet and a measurement of the abyss.

This image suggests the relation of character to the abyss of knowledge and nothingness, perhaps nothingness as knowledge. It's as if the bridge were the fiction itself, a structure built over the abyss of mortal existence. Persons can only drop an occasional measuring line into it. But the potential metaphysics of the abyss matter, in James, only as they occupy the thoughts of the fictive persons in their pragmatic human function. If *The Beast in the Jungle* offers a kind of allegory of character as emptiness, this issue is no abstraction but on the contrary experienced as a vertiginous drama of two human beings trying to make sense of their lives. That is a drama we can know, witness, and understand less in life itself than in fictions of life.

James joins Proust in exposing the dialectics of fiction and nothingness. They may both suggest to us that "character," the fictional being to whom readers attribute life and emotion and moral choice, is (a) an illusion; and (b) an inevitable and an absolutely necessary illusion, in that we are able to espouse their materiality because of their very fictionality, in a way that we could not if they were in fact "real people"; and (c) that we need fictional representations of persons in order to understand the most elusive and consequential issues of our limited human existence.

What I have said so far leads me to another line of speculation, one that reflects on the arguments of this book as a whole. The French linguist Émile Benveniste years ago considered the meaning of "subjectivity" in language.[20] He hollowed out romantic notions of subjectivity and selfhood; he consciously addressed the concept without recourse to psychology or any postulation of inwardness. Saying *I* is not the *expression* of a subjectivity. It is by saying *I* that a person *establishes* himself as subject, and everything else that we consider under the rubric "subjectivity" follows from that. Ego is first of all a property of language. For Benveniste, is *I* who says *I*. He is interested in language as discourse, as it is used in the world. When we use *I* in discourse, it necessarily implies a *you*, the person to whom our speaking is addressed. And this necessarily implies a reciprocity: the *you* in its turn becomes *I* in order to address us, and my *I* at that point becomes *you*. That reciprocity is not symmetrical: whoever says *I* at that moment is in a transcendent position, controlling the language system. But it is complementary and reversible.

It follows that *I* is a linguistic sign that has no signified—in the sense of a concept attached to it—and has as referent only the locutor currently using it. The foundation of what we call subjectivity (and hence interiority, inner depth, and all the rest) lies simply in this act of language, saying *I*, and that act is always at the same time intersubjective in that it implies a listener to the message, the *you* who in its turn can take my place as *I*. Intersubjectivity is the very condition of human speech: subjectivity is not conceivable without it. And it is the situation of speech that summons up the other distinctions of language: deictic markers (here, there) and temporal adjectives (yesterday, in the future). Verb tenses themselves, our distinctions of past, future, conditional (and refinements like the past conditional, the subjunctive, and so forth) are established in reference to the moment of speaking, what we call "the present"— which for Benveniste has no other definition than the moment in which we are speaking. That's the moment of our lives where we find ourselves.

Extrapolating from Benveniste, I want to suggest that the model of subjectivity as intersubjectivity, understood in the situation of discourse, may tell us something about narrative and our need for it. Like speech itself, narrative implies a speaker and a listener (narratologists coined the word "narratee" for symmetry with "narrator"). So what we think of as the teller's tale can't exist without it being the listener's tale as well. That fact may in some cases be clearly marked— as in the tales of Balzac and Maupassant and Saki that I discussed— or it may be merely implicit. Most novelists have ceased to speak the language of "dear reader" (other than with a sophisticated irony), but dear reader is nonetheless there in some wished-for guise or the story could not go forward. Even Dostoevsky's "underground man" speaks his monologue to someone; indeed he creates a *you* to his *I* in his very discourse. Dostoevsky 's *Notes from Underground* provide the prime instance for Mikhail Bakhtin's concept of "dialogism," which among other things means that language is by its nature dialogic: words encompassing and responding to other words. Monologues, on the stage or in a novel, necessarily imply a listener. If there is no response from a listener, they posit their own internal listener. Like Benveniste, Bakhtin demonstrates the inherently social nature of language. It is not something that "expresses" our subjectivity in the void, or in a mere echo chamber. It may be forced into situations of solitude and oppression, but it nonetheless always takes the form of aspiring to the condition of dialogue.

Can we on this basis claim that narrative is always a social act, always seeking communication, always hoping for a response from a listener? No doubt that is its intention. But that gives no special privilege to narrative and does not immunize it from unethical uses. On the contrary, because it is intended as an act of communication, narrative is subject to all the abuses of language itself. Language was given to man in order to lie, said Machiavelli; and the ability of language to use counterfactuals inhabits narrative as well. Folktales long since invented giants and fairies and magic wands and hats that make you invisible. Yet they also denounced lies and argued for the victory of human wit over the strength of monsters and the indifference of the world.

Fictional persons clearly play a key role in the communicative situation that Benveniste analyzes. They mime the dialogic relations of speaker to listener, of author to reader. They offer, explicitly or not, a model of human interaction in discourse that speaks to the desire of the text to communicate, to create a dialogue. If, as Lukács claimed, the novel is the place of the solitary individual—and reading the novel is most often an act carried on silently and alone—then the model of a communicative relation and potentially a network is crucial to its desire to be heard. "Do you see the story?" Marlow at one point asks his listeners on the *Nellie.* "Do you see anything?" Marlow goes on to claim that it is "impossible to convey the life-sensation of any given epoch of one's existence—that which makes its truth, its meaning—its subtle and penetrating essence. It is impossible. We live, as we dream—alone."[21] But Marlow's declaration of impossibility does not put a stop to his effort to communicate that "life-sensation" to his immediate audience, and beyond them to the readers of *Heart of Darkness.* Fictional persons and their effort to communicate, however difficult, however often failed, are about the central project of fictional narratives: to communicate with readers.

Fictional characters make a difference because they acknowledge and dramatize how tenuous our hold on one another is. They offer us some compensation for the lack of total communication, the blockage of full transparency, in human interaction. That's not to say that fictional beings are always easy to penetrate, or that they don't have zones of opacity that never yield to analysis, as in the case of Lucy Snowe. But we have to hand, in the novel itself, all that can be known about them, and if we are persistent readers, we will know these persons as fully as they can be known. If this represents the "escape" of fiction, a turning away from the real world, it is an escape inward, into greater knowledge and more perfect communication.

Fictional accounts of life are all about the need to hear from others—to have "counsel," in Benjamin's words—and to speak to them. What's it like to see through your eyes rather than mine—or in addition to mine? Language is an imperfect instrument of communication: "a cracked cauldron on which we beat out tunes for bears to dance to, while we would wish to move the stars to pity," Flaubert claims in *Madame Bovary*.[22] But it's what we have to hand to communicate with others, in the hope of hearing a response, of establishing a dialogue. When we fail to get a response, we try again, telling another story. We're back to Scheherazade, telling one story after another to keep alive, knowing that in the long run we are condemned but believing that in the meanwhile we need to make others hear us out.

5. What It Does

MYRIAD ARE THE ATTEMPTS to explain why we have art in general and narrative fiction in particular. Since art is of no obvious use, an adaptive biological explanation doesn't help much, though of course efforts have been made to show how art and literature benefit cognition and social adaptation.[1] I find it more productive to start from an older hypothesis: Friedrich Schiller's claim that art belongs to the "play drive," the *Spieltrieb*, which is what mediates between the form drive and the sense drive. For Schiller, the play drive keeps the other two drives in balance and produces the realm of human freedom. When form and sense work in concert, the play drive creates "living form, i.e. Beauty." Play, Schiller emphasizes, allows humans to fulfill their nature: "man only plays when he is in the fullest sense of the word a human being, and *he is only fully a human being when he plays.*"[2] That makes art the fullest realization of what it is to be human.

Glossing Schiller, we might say that the play incorporated and carried out in narrative fictions is an exercise and emblem of human freedom in that it tells about the world in ways that may prove illuminating and even useful—think back to Carlo Ginzburg's huntsman's lore—while making it clear that these fictions are fictions, the result of human fabricating and feigning (the Latin *fingo*, *fingere* includes both the made and the made up). The Borges tale

I mentioned earlier, "Tlön, Uqbar, Orbis Tertius," offers a kind of parable: if you cease to recognize that fictions are the "discipline of men, not of angels," if you start believing in them literally, they cease to be fictions and devolve into myth, which claims explanatory status and demands belief, whether it be in the "master race" or in the resurrection of the body. Fiction is playful precisely in its refusal to accept belief systems, its insistence on the "as if."

"Let's pretend" seems to be a statement and a state of mind that distinguishes humans from the so-called "higher apes."[3] Watching children do "let's pretend" games, filling imaginary teacups and driving imaginary cars, often with very few props, it is clear that while completely absorbed in making things up they are also aware that it's all make-believe. They can step out of the make-believe in order to add new props or new situations to their play; a new playmate arrives: "he can be the father"; some new object comes to hand: "let's pretend this is the engine for the train." They are, as Paul Harris puts it in *The Work of the Imagination*, in a world of "half-belief," and I think that state of mind and emotion carries over into adult enjoyment (and writing) of fictions.[4] According to Harris (and others as well), language and pretend play emerge together, along with the child's capacity to discourse of happenings that are offstage, of another time and place. Language, after all, is a useful tool in large part because it can stand in for what's not present: it's a system of signs substituting for a system of things. Much the same can be said of pretend play.

D. W. Winnicott's classic *Playing and Reality* remains for me an illuminating account of the nature and uses of play. Winnicott's observation of how in infancy we adopt "transitional objects" (a toy, a blanket—anything the infant values) leads him to define an intermediate area of experience between inner and outer reality where the child is able to respond to the world creatively, without being overwhelmed by the environment. Winnicott writes:

> Transitional objects and transitional phenomena belong to the realm of illusion which is at the basis of initiation of experience. . . . This intermediate area of experience, unchallenged in respect of its belonging to inner or external (shared) reality, constitutes the greater part of the infant's experience, and throughout life is retained in the intense experiencing that belongs to the arts and to religion and to imaginative living, and to creative scientific work.[5]

Winnicott insists, again and again, that this intermediate area, this "potential space" between me and not-me in which the infant plays, is the very precondition of adaptation to the world. He restates his insight as his "Main Thesis," which claims:

> The place where cultural experience is located is in the *potential space* between the individual and the environment (originally the object). The same can be said of playing. Cultural experience begins with creative living first manifested in play.

Play in this manner stands as the infant's original negotiation between subject and the objective world. It works because the infant is allowed (by what Winnicott calls the "good-enough mother") to believe in the illusion he or she creates in play with the transitional object, and so to obtain a sense of mastery over things.

I find Winnicott's understanding of play as the basis of imaginative living intuitively right and very useful in suggesting why we need works of the imagination of all types, both individually and in our culture. Without play, we risk being overwhelmed by an inhuman world. "Human kind cannot bear very much reality," T. S. Eliot writes in his *Four Quartets*. And Wallace Stevens says, in his *Notes Toward a Supreme Fiction*: "From this the poem springs: that we live in a place/ That is not our own and, much more, not ourselves / And hard it is in spite of blazoned days." But that is not to say that poetry, or fiction, is a turning away from the world. It is rather, like the infant's play, an attempt to find a space in which the human mind can deal with reality, speak of it, reshape it imaginatively, ask "what if" questions about it. Fictions do not overcome reality. On the contrary, as Borges's "Tlön, Uqbar, Orbis Tertius" shows us, fictions must not be confused with reality but maintained in the space of imaginative commentary on reality. In describing his work as psychotherapist, Winnicott makes the initially startling claim:

> *Psychotherapy takes place in the overlap of two areas of playing, that of the patient and that of the therapist. Psychotherapy has to do with two people playing together. The corollary of this is that where playing is not possible then the work done by the therapist is directed towards bringing the patient from a state of not being able to play into a state of being able to play.* (Italics in original)

The work of the therapist in bringing patients into a state where they can play seems to me key to the work of fictions. The traditional beginning, "Once upon a time," or alternatively, "It was a dark and stormy night," is the simplest of strategies for inducing a state of playfulness in the listener. Modern literature offers complex variations: think, for instance, of the opening of Henry James's *The Turn of the Screw*: "The story had held us, round the fire, sufficiently breathless...," which will lead to one of the listeners proposing a still more horrifying tale, a further turn of the screw. Think, too, of the disparate group of listeners on board the *Nellie*, waiting for the turn of the tide, hearing out Marlow's tale of darkness.

Winnicott's psychotherapeutic play space recalls what Freud says about the transference between patient and analyst in psychoanalysis, a space within which infantile affect is replayed in the form of repetition and acting out. These behavioral repetitions from the past point to the obsessions, repressions, and resistances that therapy must work through. Freud calls the transference a "playground" in which repetitions from the past can be understood and managed:

> The transference thus creates an intermediate region between illness and real life through which the transition from the one to the other is made. The new condition has taken over all the features of the illness; but it represents an artificial illness which is at every point accessible to our intervention. It is a piece of real experience, but one which has been made possible by especially favourable conditions, and it is of a provisional nature.[6]

That "intermediate region"—Freud's term is *Zwischenreich*—of the transference is very much like Winnicott's intermediate space of play. And Freud's "playground" (*Tummelplatz*) prepares Winnicott's claim that psychotherapy involves two people playing together. The precondition of psychoanalytic treatment and "cure" lies in the capacity to enter a space of play.

This understanding of human beings—I hesitate to say "human nature" since that implies a given which needs to be put into question—that psychoanalytic work delineates makes of all of us potential poets. As Lionel Trilling puts it, the mind according to Freud is a "poetry-making organ."[7] Jacques Lacan, rereading Freud in the context of structural linguistics, comes to similar conclusions. The condensation and displacement characteristic of dreamwork as analyzed by Freud are recast by Lacan as metaphor and metonymy, those basic functions of language. Human beings from the moment of entry into language are ready to become dreamers and fiction-makers, not to mention liars, fetishists, and perverters of the real. Our fiction-making capacity may be foundational of our search for truth in our selves and in the world, but it does not guarantee it, nor assure our mental stability. The vehicles of truth and untruth are the same. But fiction-making does seem to be crucial to the ability to carve out a space within reality for attempts at understanding and reflection.

Psychoanalysis since Freud has increasingly tended to elevate narrative to a supreme position, claiming that the analytic and therapeutic endeavor is all about getting your own story right. Freud gave us a premonition of this in his 1905 case history of "Dora" (*Fragment of an Analysis of a Case of Hysteria*):

> I begin the treatment, indeed, by asking the patient to give me the whole story of his life and illness, but even so the information I receive is never enough to let me see my way about the case. This first account may be compared to an unnavigable river whose stream is at one moment choked by masses of rock and at another divided and lost among shallows and sandbanks. I cannot help wondering how it is that the authorities can produce such smooth and precise histories in cases of hysteria. As a matter of fact the patients are incapable of

giving such reports about themselves. They can, indeed, give the physician plenty of coherent information about this or that period of their lives; but it is sure to be followed by another period as to which their communications run dry, leaving gaps unfilled, and riddles unanswered; and then again will come yet another period which will remain totally obscure and unilluminated by even a single piece of serviceable information. The connections—even the ostensible ones—are for the most part incoherent, and the sequence of different events is uncertain. Even during the course of their story patients will repeatedly correct a particular or a date, and then perhaps, after wavering for some time, return to their first version. The patients' inability to give an ordered history of their life in so far as it coincides with the history of their illness is not merely characteristic of the neurosis. It also possesses great theoretical significance.[8]

The "theoretical significance" of the patient's incoherent initial account derives from the notion that gaps and blockages result from repressions and resistances, material that is "forgotten" because too painful to recall, thus lost from memory. Trauma resists becoming part of a coherent story, although it is crucial to understanding that story.

Freud's use of the case history points to the primordial role of narrative in psychoanalytic understanding. In his early *Studies on Hysteria* he confesses his surprise at how much his case presentations read like short stories—and goes on to claim that story is the only way to get at the development and manifestation of symptoms and to recover their causes. Hysteria emerges in time, even though it manifests itself as the blockage of forward movement, in the symbolic fixation of trauma as bodily symptom. The course of the analysis seeks to restore a sense of cause and effect, to put time back into gear, so that the story can move forward. The patient should eventually be able to recover a workable sense of her own life story and its future possibilities. The case history tells an exemplary story: the unfolding story of an individual in all her particularity that stands for a class of stories, that illustrates a classic instance of narrative.

Freud's case histories claim to uncover a past history that needs to be integrated into the present, though the status of this history becomes more complicated in Freud's later thinking. In the case of the Wolf Man (*From the History of an Infantile Neurosis*) he debates whether the infant Sergei P. really did witness his parents copulating—the "primal scene" that he never actually recalled but that was reconstructed by analyst and patient from the traumatic wolf dream. Was it instead a "primal fantasy"? The discussion is inconclusive: Freud believes that in this case it was real but that a fantasy could just as well be the source of trauma. He returns to the case in one of his last essays on technique, "Constructions in Analysis" (1937), in which he argues that the purpose of the analyst remains the same as that articulated in "Dora": "What we are in search of is a picture of the patient's forgotten years that shall be alike trustworthy and in all essential respects complete." Yet here he factors in a considerably more problematic and partial recovery of that picture of those forgotten years. If the work of the analyst is to construct elements of a past narrative that the patient then ratifies (or refuses, leading the analyst to discard certain hypotheses), it happens that:

> The path that starts from the analyst's construction ought to end in the patient's recollection; but it does not always lead so far. Quite often we do not succeed in bringing the patient to recollect what

has been repressed. Instead of that, if the analysis is carried out correctly, we produce in him an assured conviction of the truth of the construction which achieves the same therapeutic result as a recaptured memory.[9]

Here Freud's concession that the story produced in analysis may not be a full recovery of the patient's history takes on the air of an assertion. The credibility and therapeutic value of the narrative does not consist in its absolute fidelity to past history but rather in its persuasiveness. All we need is an "assured conviction" of the truth of the story. It must have happened this way because of the results it produced. That sounds like storytelling in the late Henry James or Virginia Woolf or William Faulkner more than those, such as Arnold Bennett, whom Woolf labeled "Edwardians." Freud enlists himself with narrative modernists.

While Freud remains committed to getting the story right, to using construction only to fill in missing pieces of the "forgotten years," in his wake some psychoanalysts have gone further, making the claim that the factuality of the story constructed between patient and analyst has no importance, that what matters is only the story itself, its capacity to create therapeutic conviction.[10] The power of the story to make sense of a life is all that matters. An extreme version of this position has become characteristic of some work in narrative analysis (on autobiography, for instance) and in psychology. In Jerome Bruner, for example:

I want to begin by proposing boldly that, in effect, there is no such thing as an intuitively obvious and essential self to know, one that just sits there ready to be portrayed in words. Rather, we constantly construct and reconstruct our selves to meet the needs of the situations we encounter, and we do so with the guidance of our memories of the past and our hopes and fears for the future. Telling oneself about oneself is like making up a story about who and what we are, what's happened, and why we're doing what we're doing.[11]

As stated, this seems uncontroversial: we do narrate ourselves to ourselves, constantly relocating ourselves in an ongoing story. But this narrativist position can modulate into Galen Strawson's "fallacy of our age," as when Bruner states elsewhere: "In the end, we *become* the autobiographical narratives by which we 'tell about' our lives." Or as Oliver Sacks claims: "This narrative *is* us, our identities."[12] We may wish our self-narrative to be us, but that seems an excessively idealist or even solipsist position in that our discourse of ourselves comes up against all sorts of reversals of fortune, including disease and death, that contest our capacity to control the narrative.

Paul Ricoeur proposes a useful distinction: we are narrators but not authors of our lives. He argues that "a life *examined*, in the sense borrowed from Socrates, is a life *narrated*." That puts our narratives of our lives on the side of analytic reflection rather than the living itself. He argues eloquently that mimesis understood as the representation of reality should not suggest a kind of reproduction or doubling of the real object but rather the "cut that opens the space of fiction."[13] Fiction is a place of understanding. This may offer an indirect confirmation of Benjamin's claim that we seek in the *stories of others* some illumination of our own "shivering lives." As self-aware self narrators, we must recognize the inadequacy of our narratives to solve our own and other's problems. We may resemble far too much Frédéric and his pal in Flaubert's *Sentimental Education*, who end up comforting themselves with stories about the failure of their lives. As Lukács suggests, it is memory and stories retrieved from memory that provide a struggle with time that is unremitting but always defeated.

Time is a problem for the human species in ways that space is not. We are mortal, time-bound in a more dire way than place-bound. Ricoeur has given the most extensive study of the way the human experience of time is reconfigured in narrative, arguing that "time becomes human to the extent that it is articulated in a narrative mode, and that narrative gains its full meaning when it becomes a condition of temporal existence." Many a novel is about changing places, moving from province to city, wandering in space, seeking adventures along the road. But time is an insoluble problem. The limits it imposes on human existence are built into the substance of the novel, as it records changes in the lives of its imagined persons. This may lead to a final distribution of praise and blame, punishment and reward, as in the final pages of many a Dickens novel, but then again it may, as in *Villette*, give us a more problematic understanding of the interplay of time, life, and telling. The most ambitious attempt to deal with temporality, Proust's *In Search of Lost Time*, concludes with the protagonist deciding to write a book that will have the "shape of time" but simultaneously asking himself if he has enough time to bring it to fruition. The figure of Scheherazade appears once again, telling stories under the threat of extinction.

To insist that we are only the stories we tell about ourselves takes an important truth and trivializes it—which seems to be something of a constant in the story about narrative that I have been trying to tell. The great novelists have recognized that life needs to be shaped and understood through narrative. But they have also understood the limits to the order that fiction can impose on life. The novel became the dominant form that it is with the secularization of thought, which entailed the notion that we need to work out the meanings of our lives here and now, not in some large sacred scheme of things that will redeem time in eternity. The capaciousness of the novel made it the ideal vehicle for searching after that meaning of life that Benjamin claims we miss, and long for, in our secular solitude. And the dominance of the novel has been accompanied by the critique that its search for form is unfaithful to the experience of life, which is formless, which never reaches the finality of meaning. Sartre's dissent from the dominant narrative paradigm distinguishes telling from living. His fictional spokesman Roquentin in *Nausea* argues that when you tell a story—as opposed to living it—you only appear to begin at the beginning, since in reality "the end is there, transforming everything."[14] When you open a novel you know that its ending lies in wait, making its hero live the details of the present "as annunciations, as promises . . . blind and deaf to all that did not herald adventure"; "we forget that the future wasn't yet there." The novelistic person necessarily is part of an "adventure," which in its Latin root, *ad-venire*, refers us to what is to come. Accordingly, Sartre came to reject the novel (much as today's "autofictionalists" have done) as a falsification of the contingency of reality that blinds us to our freedom and what he sees as the obligation to choose our becoming at every moment.

Is it possible that we should see narrative form as a lie? This would mean that those like Bruner who claim we are our narratives threaten to take us over the brink into delusion, into a belief in our demiurgic capacity to order reality as we like. Such a possibility does not seem to me reason to abandon narrativity, however: we still need to try to find order and meaning in our lives and in the flow of passing time. But I think understanding narrative as a condition of meaningfulness in time implies also that we live in the awareness that narrative, as Borges says of Tlön, is the discipline of men, not of angels. There is only so much that storytelling can achieve in the struggle with temporality and the eventual victory of mortality. As I have argued, one must use fictions always with the awareness of their fictionality. They are "as if" constructions of reality that we need, that we have to use creatively in order not to die of the chaos of reality—but they are not reality itself.[15]

Everything we have learned about play, from Schiller and Winnicott and others, argues that it creates a space between self and world that brings satisfaction because it liberates us from the laws of necessity—for the time it lasts. Recent work by "evocritics" on the adaptive function of art, including storytelling, may or may not be persuasive: for me, it often resembles the just-so story in explaining a current situation (an elephant has a trunk) by a story of the reasons trunks made elephants more adaptive to their habitat ("how the elephant got its trunk").[16] The explanation depends in a tautological manner on the characteristics of what's to be explained. Nonetheless, the claim that storytelling plays a role in our adaptation to reality seems true enough. As the Darwinist Joseph Carroll writes: "Literature and the other arts are devices of orientation, like compasses, sextants, and sonar, and they are vital to personal development, to the integration of individual identities within a cultural order, and to the imaginative adjustment of the individual to the whole larger world in which he or she lives."[17] Narrative fictions offer lessons learned from the past and ways to think about what lies ahead. The kind of imaginative play they use and inculcate may make us more alert to our surroundings, their dangers and potentialities: that is part of my claim that narrative is a cognitive instrument.

More specifically illuminating in my view is work on early childhood play and creativity that demonstrates that the capacity and desire for make-believe manifest themselves very early in life—for Winnicott, from the very beginning, in the transitional space between infant and mother. For psychologist Paul Harris, the child's disposition toward fictions emerges along with speech itself, around age two. By fictions, he means (as I do) make-believe that is aware of its make-believe status, that is capable of holding simultaneously belief in the fiction and awareness of reality. Children know how to use counterfactuals, they experience emotion in playing even while aware that the source of the emotion is fictive. They are capable of what Harris calls a "subjective displacement" into the play world.

That is to say that the fiction-making capacity of humans seems to be there from very early on. It's not something learned later in life, and it's not a kind of add-on to basic knowledge acquisition skills. Bruner, I noted earlier, claims that young children don't so much learn as budding scientists—practicing experiments to discover empirical truths—but rather through the exchange of stories, true or untrue. How to deal with the parental world and then the more extensive world of adults lies at the heart of much early make-believe. How to explain current factual and emotional reality takes form as stories. There are the stories and theories about sexuality and sexual difference that Freud brought to our attention: stories that confront the riddle of the sphinx by ingenious fictions that will be constantly revised as the child grows older, even as what we think of as adult sexuality will continue to be tinged with infan-

tile scenarios of satisfaction. The child's explanatory fictions become
the adult's driving fantasies. One result of the child's early investment
in fiction seems to be the endurance of fantasy later in life. We are
all fictionalists, including of our own lives.

The philosopher Charles Taylor claims that we are part of "webs
of interlocution," echoing Benveniste, who describes discourse as
fundamentally intersubjective. Taylor makes the interlocutionary
situation constitutive of our lives as social and ethical beings, necessarily interacting with others and determined by that interaction.[18]
This looks back to the Kantian adage that other people are not to
be used merely instrumentally, to serve our own ends, but must be
regarded as autonomous ethical beings in their own right. The
weight of that "must" is of course open to question, since we daily
see violations of it in a world full of selfish manipulation and seduc-
tion. The novel is full of such abusers of power; they figure promi-
nently in its pages, along with their victims and at times chastisers.
Questions of the wrong and right ways of treating other people are
everywhere in the novel. It's the very form for addressing such conflicts, as virtually every major novelist makes evident, from Richardson to Tolstoy to Proust to Coetzee and Ishiguro. Henry James
seems to me in many ways the supreme novelist of human relations.
His greatest fascination and fear is how people manipulate others,
as Isabel Archer is manipulated by Gilbert Osmond, little Maisie
Farange by the whole adult world, Milly Theale by Kate Croy—the
list could be continued. For James, as for many other novelists, to
manipulate another, to use someone for your own ends, is to deny
that person his or her freedom, an irreducible definition of the
human. To deprive another of freedom is the supreme ethical

fault. It is also, for the novelist, as James conceives that practitioner, a kind of technical and aesthetic fault. The novelist owes his created persons a grant of freedom so that they may develop their full potential.

That is a position articulated over and over by James, in his essay "The Future of the Novel," for instance, and in "The Lesson of Balzac," where his whipping boy is W. M. Thackeray and his insistence that the heroine of his *Vanity Fair*, Becky Sharp, always be held under the ferule of moral judgment, so that the reader sees her only as an example of censurable behavior rather than as a being in herself. In contrast to Thackeray's treatment of Becky stands Balzac's of the awful Valérie Marneffe in *Cousin Bette* (*La Cousine Bette*). "*Balzac aime sa Valérie*," writes James, quoting from Hippolyte Taine: he loves this character. James goes on:

> It was just through this love of each seized identity, and of the sharpest and liveliest identities most, that Madame Marneffe's creator was able to marshal his array at all. The love, as we call it, the joy in their communicated and exhibited movement, in their standing on their feet and going of themselves and acting out their characters, was what rendered possible the saturation that I speak of; what supplied him, through the inevitable gaps of his preparation and the crevices of his prison, his long prison of labor, a short cut to the knowledge he required. It was by loving them—as the terms of his subject and the nuggets of his mine—that he knew them; it was not by knowing that he loved....
>
> It all comes back, in fine, to that respect for the liberty of the subject which I should be willing to name as *the* great sign of the painter of the first order.[19]

I quote James at such length because I believe the point he makes is crucial not only to his preference of Balzac over Thackeray, and not only to his own practice of the novel, but to the novel itself as genre.

That's not to say that novels aren't full of manipulative characters who try and often succeed in using others to their own ends, or that the novel necessarily promotes the triumph of the free spirits. Nor is it to claim that all novelists subscribe to James's prescription of respect for the "liberty of the subject." They may manipulate their characters as fully as Thackeray, if less obviously. Sartre famously complained this was the case in the novels of François Mauriac, wrapping up his indictment with the words: "God is not a novelist; M. François Mauriac isn't either."[20] Yet the novel, the least rule-governed of literary forms ("lawless," André Gide called it), is the most adaptable to any and all situations; it possesses a vertiginous freedom that James believes should dictate its method as well as its themes.

Novelists value the novel for this absence of constraining rules. But that freedom can seem excessive. In his autobiography, *The Words* (*Les Mots*), Sartre describes how as a precocious budding novelist creating a continuing serial fiction, he discovered the immense and arbitrary power of the novelist. He could kill his heroine Daisy in the next episode.[21] Or he could put out her eyes and have her wake up blind. He found this power frightening; its application was arbitrary, an unmerited and capricious imposition of constraint on existence. Any novelist must feel something like Sartre's fright at his power over life. I recall from writing two novels of my own the overwhelming sense of possibilities and choices every morning when I set to writing. Balzac felt something similar: his work contains many tales of artists and scientists and thinkers undone and driven insane by their search for power and control over life. But still, when you open the covers of a new novel, it is in a sense of anticipation of the ways it will expand and open up your single life in liberating ways. As James said in advice to aspiring writers of the novel: "Give it its head, and let it range."[22]

This valuation of the novel as a place of unconstraint, free to treat all subjects as it sees fit and in its freedom of treatment very often about that freedom as well, has something to do with what Taylor calls the "affirmation of ordinary life."[23] As literature ceased to be the story of epic heroes and divine allegories, that is, with the coming of modernity and the dominance of the novel, everyday life, the ordinary, emerged as its central concern. Rousseau in his "Second Preface" to his one novel, which became the runaway best-seller of the French eighteenth century, calls attention to the banality of his characters, their milieu, and their activities. This *Conversation on Novels* (*Entretien sur les romans*) takes the form of a dialogue between the author and his reader, who complains: "What's the point of keeping a register of what everyone can see every day in his house or that of his neighbor?"[24] This reproach of fidelity to the everyday is of course taken by Rousseau as a compliment rather than a criticism, to which he happily responds: this is not a novel. It's rather a collection of letters (an epistolary novel) that shows humans as they really are. That also explains why it goes on for so long: it takes time to know the characters—their faults, their virtues, their whole lives. Rousseau writes a polemical defense of what would become known, nearly a century later, as "realism": everyday life as the subject of fiction.

This capacity of the novel to explore the everyday and to make its relationships and events subjects of a reader's interest depends, I think, on the same human faculty that children demonstrate in play. Both are about the creation of a space of freedom within the inexorable mechanisms of the real. That play, in the case of the successful fiction, delivers us back to reality changed, enhanced, with a greater wisdom in our stock. Such has been the claim of serious novelists for many centuries. They respond to critiques that fault the novel for turning away from reality with the claim that this detour through fiction will tell you more about reality than you know, and give you greater understanding of the stakes of the way you live your life. The emergence of language and the emergence of the ability to invent imaginary situations, fictions, Paul Harris suggests, somehow fused during the evolution of *Homo sapiens.* What we are now are not only creatures of language but creatures of our imaginative constructs as well. The novel effectively serves those constructs.

My argument in this book has ranged, and digressed, over different uses and abuses of narrative, across a number of discursive communities. Where has it come out? Possibly with something fairly obvious, but nonetheless worth repeating. We have fictions in order not to die of the forlornness of our condition in the world. That fiction-making is a form of play that is crucial to our survival because it is crucial to our capacity to understand our place in the world. The capacity to speak fictionally, in an imaginative "as if," forms part of human language capability. It may be that all language is unrelated to the real, solely a house that humans have built in order to shelter within the real. That we cannot determine. But to the extent we have language, we necessarily have fictions, good and bad, as part of our discursive capability.

Good and bad: there is no guarantee that fictions will further human flourishing. We do not need to look far back in history to see what happens when certain fictions gain the status of dominant and all-explaining myths. Especially, perhaps, those myths that arise from resentment, from the sense of social exclusion or powerlessness. The unscrupulous seekers after power—who currently appear to outnumber those who seek power to do justice—promote and possibly themselves believe myths that enable their takeover and their exercise of totalitarian power. Critique of their myths goes forward but often seems to make no difference. I began by quoting Tyrion, bestowing rule on Bran in *Game of Thrones*, and I return to it: "There's nothing in the world more powerful than a good story. Nothing can stop it. No enemy can defeat it." True, alas. Lawful regimes crumble before the too-good story. Populations become largely submissive.

Story is powerful, and for that reason it demands a powerful critical response. We need to dismantle and contest its claims to totalistic explanatory force. In this simple recognition we loop back to where we began. Stories, narrative fictions, have no positive or negative valence of themselves. They can be used as tools to advance the worse as well as the better cause. We should celebrate the human capacity to imagine, to create other worlds, while retaining our skeptical capacities. We will and must continue to tell and to listen to stories— but I plead for a more attentive and critical attitude toward them. Stories are tricky, and often designed to be so. We need to be on guard. At the same time, within a society and an educational establishment more and more dominated by a commitment to "useful" and instrumental knowledge, we need to assert how crucial the spirit of play still is to human development. In Wallace Stevens's words:

Light the first light of evening, as in a room
In which we rest and, for small reason, think
The world imagined is the ultimate good.[25]

Placing the "world imagined" in balance between "small reason" and "ultimate good," Stevens seems to leave us just about in the right place. Asserting the reason of fictions against the darkness, while remaining on our guard against their capacity for ruin, seems to be where we come out.

6. Further Thoughts
Stories in and of the Law

EVER SINCE THERE HAVE BEEN LITIGANTS and courts, the law has been full of stories. In pleadings and arguments and judgments, law makes use of narrative constantly—yet rarely with any recognition that its narrative commitments need analytic attention. The myriad roles of storytelling in the law constitute a kind of legal repressed unconscious: that which exists but has not been analyzed, and indeed not often thought in need of analysis. The expressed attitude of judges and lawyers toward story is most often one of contempt, which may harbor as well a certain fear: if stories in the law were to get out of hand there would be trouble, probably in the form of emotional turmoil. Much of courtroom procedure is designed to keep stories within bounds. Cross-examination breaks up stories, subjects them to the questioning attorney's template of how he or she wants the story to run. The courtroom will often generate opposing stories, or possibly a dominant story that is challenged, its component parts and their combination put into doubt by the opposing party, which seeks to undermine its overall coherence. When there is an appeal of the decision reached in the courtroom, it may take be presented as a critique of the form given to the winning story, and sometimes the proposal of a better one.

This pervasive yet unanalyzed prevalence of story in the law could be approached in many different ways.[1] I want here to talk about two: the making of narrative of "the facts," how they are styled and the effect they make; and the narratives produced when Supreme Court opinions reflect on the histories of constitutional interpretation.

Facts and Stories in the Law

Facts described in narrative form: that is in essence Louis O. Mink's description of the historian's task. It's easy to recognize that legal adjudication has a similar task, though the facts tend to be more recent than those told by the historian, and the purpose of putting them into narrative form is not simply to say what happened but to decide what to do about what happened: whether and how to assign blame, how to arrive at conviction. Conviction in two senses: the jury must reach a conviction of the truth of the story for the accused to be convicted of a crime. The investigation or inquest begins with the facts on the ground, and that is what law will have to deal with in the courtroom. And beyond: if the case goes up to an appellate court, those facts will be retold in an effort to judge whether the law has been correctly applied to them—whether those facts were appropriately formalized. But what are "the facts"? Is there any way to know them independent of their description in narrative form? Though there may be some facts that appear to stand alone—for instance, those produced by scientific testing—in most cases the determination of what's a relevant fact, even in expert testimony, is bound up with a narrative hypothesis, most simply stated as "what one is looking for."

Facts become perspicuous as what we call "clues," facts that once connected in a linked chain tell a story. Sherlock Holmes in one of his later cases complains to Dr. Watson: "Your fatal habit of looking at everything from the point of view of a story instead of as a scientific exercise has ruined what might have been an instructive and even classical series of demonstrations."[2] Holmes claims he would prefer to see his methodology distilled into a one-volume scientific textbook, a grumpy critique of the very thing that makes his work famous. This exchange between the inseparable partners in the pursuit of crime points to the inseparability of detection from *story*; it can take form only as a narrative that aligns facts, understood as clues, to reach a solution.

In the course of criminal legal proceedings, several narratives of the facts of the case occur, from the opening statement of the prosecution about what it intends to prove, to the closing arguments that summarize the conflicting versions of what happened. And on to the summary of what was discovered and proved at trial that will be given by an appellate court if the case continues. The statement of facts in the appellate opinion is often the best way to understand what is at stake in the case, since the appellate judge gives a succinct and pertinent presentation of the facts as they have been determined by the trial court, by what the law calls the "trier of fact": usually the jury, or, in a bench trial, the judge. So I begin this exploration of narrative in the law with a classic appellate opinion.

In the case of *People v. Zackowitz* (1930), the opinion of the New York Court of Appeals was written by its chief judge, Benjamin Cardozo. There has been a shooting in Brooklyn, and the victim, Frank Coppola, is dead. Cardozo states at the outset: "A crime is admitted. What is doubtful is the degree only." Then he gives us his account of the facts:

> Four young men, of whom Coppola was one, were at work repairing an automobile in a Brooklyn street. A woman, the defendant's wife, walked by on the opposite side. One of the men spoke to her insultingly, or so at least she understood him. The defendant, who had dropped behind to buy a newspaper, came up to find his wife in tears. He was told she had been insulted, though she did not then repeat the words. Enraged, he stepped across the street and upbraided the offenders with words of coarse profanity. He informed them, so the survivors testify, that "if they did not get out of there in five minutes, he would come back and bump them all off." Rejoining his wife, he walked with her to their apartment house located close at hand. He was heated with liquor which he had been drinking at a dance. Within the apartment he induced her to tell him what the insulting words had been. A youth had asked her to lie with him, and had offered her two dollars. With rage aroused again, the defendant went back to the scene of the insult and found the four young men still working at the car. In a statement to the police, he said that he had armed himself at the apartment with a twenty-five calibre automatic pistol. In his testimony at the trial he said that this pistol had been in his pocket all the evening. Words and blows followed, and then a shot. The defendant kicked Coppola in the stomach. There is evidence that Coppola went for him with a wrench. The pistol came from the pocket, and from the pistol a single shot, which did its deadly work. The defendant walked away and at the corner met his wife who had followed him from the home. The two took

a taxicab to Manhattan where they spent the rest of the night at the dwelling of a friend. On the way the defendant threw his pistol into the river. He was arrested on January 7, 1930, about two months following the crime.[3]

No wonder Cardozo is considered one of the great legal stylists: this is quick, it's vivid, it's even funny. There is a kind of arch distance between the eminent jurist and the low-life characters in this Brooklyn brawl (rewrite, for instance, "A youth had asked her to lie with him" in the probable words used by the youth). In fact, the speed and concision of the narrative make Cardozo's doctrinal point: that the conviction of Joseph Zackowitz for first-degree murder cannot stand. There was no premeditation, no malice aforethought, but simply a violent reaction to a situation of confrontation. The efforts of the district attorney at trial to characterize Zackowitz as a "man murderously inclined," someone with a propensity to crime, cannot stand up to analysis.

The most stunning line in Cardozo's narrative is: "The pistol came from the pocket, and from the pistol a single shot, which did its deadly work." You can imagine a cartoon version in which that pistol just rises from the pocket and shoots. No finger on the trigger. No agency. That's the point Cardozo wishes to insist on: the shooting was simply the result of the heated confrontation. The prosecution's claim that Zackowitz kept several weapons in his apartment is irrelevant and prejudicial. We are not to load a criminal defendant with "propensity evidence," tending to demonstrate he had a character that was bound to commit a crime. What is needed is proof specific to the act to be judged by the jury. In what may be the most important doctrinal line of his opinion, Cardozo states: "In a very real sense a defendant starts his life afresh when he stands before a jury, a prisoner at the bar." The past is irrelevant. The pertinent narrative should concern only the immediate circumstances of the deed and its motivation. The trial court erred in setting Zackowitz's actions in a larger biographical frame, and since it did, Zackowitz must be granted a new trial.

I think Cardozo gets it right in *Zackowitz*; in some other cases, such as the torts case *Palsgraf v. Long Island Railroad Company*, his concise and rapid narrative seems to me to obscure rather than clarify crucial facts on the ground, and to reach the wrong conclusion.[4] My point here is that his narrative of that night in Brooklyn alone virtually makes the rest of his opinion unnecessary. The story as told has already made an argument about Zackowitz's innocence of the charge of premeditated homicide. Cardozo's telling of the facts is enough to make his judgment. He bears out the radical claim, mentioned in my first chapter, of Anthony Amsterdam, a lawyer, and Jerome Bruner, a psychologist, that the traditional supposition that the law could proceed by "examining free-standing factual data selected on grounds of their logical pertinency" is not tenable. They write: "Increasingly we are coming to recognize that both the questions and the answers in such matters of 'fact' depend largely upon one's choice (considered or unconsidered) of some overall narrative as best describing *what happened* or *how the world works*."[5]

I largely agree with such an analysis: facts come to life and become significant only when ordered in a narrative, and the generic contours of that narrative often weigh heavily in the choice of those facts—or, at least, those facts and that narrative are coproduced. But I don't think many judges or other legal actors recognize that their choice of narrative may shape their selection and alignment of the facts on the ground. "Just the facts" remains the accepted legal common sense, with little analytic attention to the plotting of their presentation. I know of only one opinion of the US Supreme Court that addresses how narrative may shape a criminal case: that of Justice David Souter in *Old Chief v. United States* (1997). Justice Souter riffs on what he calls "narrative integrity," the need for a jury to hear a case in all its fullness, without omissions: it is story that persuades, and it convinces jurors that they can pass judgment in confidence that they have understood what happened and what it means. Souter writes:

> A syllogism is not a story, and a naked proposition in a courtroom may be no match for the robust evidence that would be used to prove it. People who hear stories interrupted by gaps of abstraction may be puzzled at the missing chapters. . . . A convincing tale can be told with economy, but when economy becomes a break in the natural sequence of narrative evidence, an assurance that the missing link is really there is never more than second best.[6]

Souter argues persuasively that it is narrative rather than other forms of presentation of "the facts" that undergirds the difficult act of passing judgment in confidence that it is right to do so:

> When a juror's duty does seem hard, the evidentiary account of what a defendant has thought and done can accomplish what no set of abstract statements ever could, not just to prove a fact but to establish its human significance, and so to implicate the law's moral underpinnings and a juror's obligation to sit in judgment.

Yet it is because he understands the power of narrative that Souter comes to the decision that the evidence of defendant Johnny Lynn Old Chief's prior conviction—on a crime very similar to the present charge—must be excluded. Following the same logic as Cardozo's claim that a defendant starts his life afresh at trial, Souter insists that the earlier crime belongs to another story, a closed chapter in Old Chief's existence. To link the present alleged crime to the defendant's past criminal activity, he says, may "overpersuade" a jury, convincing it that Old Chief, like Zackowitz, is someone of murderous propensity.

In its insistence that the act, not the person, be judged, the law generally finds life stories both irrelevant and dangerous. Souter's opinion reflects eloquently on the potency of story in the law, but in order to restrict the uses of narrative. Since story is so forceful, the law needs to police and cabin its uses. In practice, this has tended to mean a kind of willful blindness to the importance of narrative in the law. When legal theorists such as Judge Richard Posner acknowledge the role of stories in the law it is most often to treat them with suspicion, as an uncontrollable kind of discourse, and Souter's considered reflections on narrative have been largely ignored in subsequent Supreme Court decisions.[7]

Still, any courtroom lawyer must know that she or he needs to present the jury with a coherent story of what happened, and that story is likely to take a conventional form, with standard motivations, acts, and outcomes. It cannot be otherwise, since we live in a world of stories, which we use to account for everyday life, and especially our own lives.[8] As novelists have always known, and as psychologists have known at least since Freud, the lack of a more or less coherent narrative of one's life indicates psychic blockage, confusion, the inability to understand one's identity, an incapacity to move forward. We saw that Freud stated the problem early on in his case history of "Dora": "This first account [given by the patient] may be compared to an unnavigable river whose stream is at one moment choked by masses of rock and at another divided and lost among shallows and sandbanks." If one were to ban narrative from the courtroom, there could be no more verdicts. Crime and punishment demand stories.

It is strange, then, that the law has not seen the need to articulate and formalize its understanding of narrative and the rules of storytelling, both in the courtroom and in appellate opinions, where the story that has imposed itself at trial is retold in order to judge whether the legal rules have been followed, whether the facts have been correctly presented to the jury. In *Zackowitz*, the story retold in the court of appeals—and such retellings can take us up several levels, ultimately to the Supreme Court—makes clear how the telling shapes what is told. A number of Fourth Amendment "search and seizure" cases are especially revealing: a search is by its nature narrative. The question in *Florida v. Jardines* (2013), for instance, is whether the use of a trained dog brought onto the porch of a house in order to sniff for marijuana violates the ban on "unreasonable" searches.[9] Here is Justice Antonin Scalia writing for the majority that found the search illegal:

In 2006, Detective William Pedraja of the Miami-Dade Police Department received an unverified tip that marijuana was being grown in the home of respondent Joelis Jardines. One month later, the Department and the Drug Enforcement Administration sent a joint surveillance team to Jardines' home. Detective Pedraja was part of that team. He watched the home for fifteen minutes and saw no vehicles in the driveway or activity around the home, and could not see inside because the blinds were drawn. Detective Pedraja then approached Jardines' home accompanied by Detective Douglas Bartelt, a trained canine handler who had just arrived at the scene with his drug-sniffing dog. The dog was trained to detect the scent of marijuana, cocaine, heroin, and several other drugs, indicating the presence of any of these substances through particular behavioral changes recognizable by his handler.

In contrast, see the version of the story told by Justice Samuel Alito, dissenting:

> According to the Court . . . the police officer in this case, Detective Bartelt, committed a trespass because he was accompanied during his otherwise lawful visit to the front door of respondent's house by his dog, Franky. Where is the authority evidencing such a rule? Dogs have been domesticated for about 12,000 years; they were ubiquitous in both this country and Britain at the time of the adoption of the Fourth Amendment; and their acute sense of smell has been used in law enforcement for centuries.

Bartelt and his faithful pet Franky have every right to come visiting on Jardines' front porch. How can Scalia be so upset about it? And the argument goes on, evoking on the one hand customary visits to one's front door—mailman, Girl Scouts selling cookies—versus the violation of "curtilage," the area around the home in which one can have a reasonable expectation of privacy, on the other. Curtilage, the dictionary tells us, derives from the Anglo-French *curtillage*, the enclosed land belonging to a house, or the kitchen garden, which is itself from Old French *cortillage* (kitchen garden), from *cortil* (garden), and ultimately from Latin *cohort-*, *cohors* (farmyard). We are dealing with an ancient story of private space that Scalia finds trespassed by the sniffing Franky. And I note that Scalia's insistence on trespass leads Justice Elena Kagan, who concurs in his opinion, to write separately in order to foreground another story: the more general story of the invasion of privacy, a story Scalia wishes to avoid because of its possible far-reaching consequences in other matters (abortion rights, for instance) but which Kagan sees as far more important than the property trespass at the center of Scalia's story.

The three divergent opinions by Scalia, Kagan, and Alito are of course concerned—as Supreme Court opinions always are—with precedent: using precedents and setting precedents. Especially when we are talking about whether a search and seizure is "unreasonable" according to the Fourth Amendment, precedents almost always take story form: they are narrative templates for judging what's allowed. A search requires a story: even when police apply for a search warrant they tell a story of how and where they will search, and what they think they will find. So when courts analyze the legality of the search, they inevitably engage in a kind of narrative analysis. The "reasonability" of the search depends on its narrative plausibility.

Take as another example *Utah v. Strieff* (2016). Detective Fackrell had staked out a house in South Salt Lake City on the basis of an anonymous tip that drugs were being dealt there. When defendant Strieff left the house after a short visit, Fackrell stopped him. He then "requested Strieff's identification, and Strieff produced his Utah identification card. Officer Fackrell relayed Strieff's information to a police dispatcher, who reported that Strieff had an out-standing arrest warrant for a traffic violation. Officer Fackrell then arrested Strieff pursuant to that warrant. When Officer Fackrell searched Strieff incident to the arrest, he discovered a baggie of methamphetamine and drug paraphernalia."[10] At trial, the prose-cution conceded that the "stop" of Strieff was illegal: there was no known arrest warrant, no probable cause, no consent to be searched. But the drug evidence was allowed on the grounds that the discovery of a valid arrest warrant (for a wholly different incident) "attenuated" the illegality of the search. The Utah Supreme Court reversed Strieff's conviction. But the US Supreme Court, in an opinion writ-ten by Justice Clarence Thomas, reinstated the conviction on the grounds of the attenuation provided by the warrant.

This story is then retold by an angry Justice Sonia Sotomayor, dissenting:

> The Court today holds that the discovery of a warrant for an unpaid parking ticket will forgive a police officer's violation of your Fourth Amendment rights. Do not be soothed by the opinion's technical language: This case allows the police to stop you on the street, demand your identification, and check it for outstanding traffic warrants—even if you are doing nothing wrong. If the officer discovers a warrant for a fine you forgot to pay, courts will now excuse his illegal stop and will admit into evidence anything he happens to find by searching you after arresting you on the warrant. Because the Fourth Amend-ment should prohibit, not permit, such misconduct, I dissent.

Sotomayor rewrites Thomas's narrative of the honest mistake made by Officer Fackrell, redeemed by the discovery of the outstanding arrest warrant, as an apocalyptic future story (which is itself something of a genre in judicial opinions): if you understand Thomas's story fully, you will see that it produces a future dystopia of citizens routinely bullied by illegal police stops, justified retrospectively by outstanding warrants that, Sotomayor goes on to note, are terrifyingly common in the United States: "The Department of Justice recently reported that in the town of Ferguson, Missouri, with a population of 21,000, 16,000 people had outstanding warrants against them. In Newark, New Jersey, officers stopped 52,235 pedestrians within a 4-year period and ran warrant checks on 39,308 of them. (Dept. of Justice, Civil Rights Div., Investigation of the Newark Police Department 8, 19, n. 15 [2014])."

By the end of her opinion, Sotomayor brings the Fourth Amendment stories into real-life American communities, and especially those of minority groups, and in doing so evokes some of the most powerful narratives written about race and class:

> This case involves a *suspicionless* stop, one in which the officer initiated this chain of events without justification. As the Justice Department notes... many innocent people are subjected to the humiliations of these unconstitutional searches. The white defendant in this case shows that anyone's dignity can be violated in this manner. See M. Gottschalk, Caught 119–138 (2015). But it is no secret that people of color are disproportionate victims of this type of scrutiny. See M. Alexander, The New Jim Crow 95–136 (2010). For generations, black and brown parents have given their children "the talk"—instructing them never to run down the street; always keep your hands where they can be seen; do not even think of talking back to a stranger—all out of fear of how an officer with a gun will

react to them. See, *e.g.*, W. E. B. Du Bois, The Souls of Black Folk
(1903); J. Baldwin, The Fire Next Time (1963); T. Coates, Between
the World and Me (2015).

By legitimizing the conduct that produces this double consciousness, this case tells everyone, white and black, guilty and innocent,
that an officer can verify your legal status at any time. It says that
your body is subject to invasion while courts excuse the violation of
your rights. It implies that you are not a citizen of a democracy but
the subject of a carceral state, just waiting to be cataloged.

Sotomayor has upped the ante of the story of Strieff's arrest, and in
doing so has greatly widened the narrative circle. She has made this
one case speak to the larger American tragedy of racial inequity,
oppressive policing, and mass incarceration of minority citizens.
Though she did not win the argument in *Utah v. Strieff*, her story
continues to have resonance and force well beyond the confines of
the case. And perhaps someday it will be cited in a case with a more
enlightened and comprehensive result.

Supreme Court narratives are of special importance because they
establish precedents and, through the police power of the state,
shape reality directly. "It is so ordered," the opinion of the Court
typically concludes. That final order makes blatant the performative
nature of all legal speech: the decisions it arrives at are not simply
constative, they impose themselves on reality. They send people to
prison, even to death, or else free them from the constraint of legal
process. And so too the narratives told—retold—at the highest

appellate level themselves possess a performative force. "It is so ordered": the story as we have told it orders reality decisively. This is what happened—nothing else—and all the consequences follow. Dissenters of course are free to protest, to claim that the majority's narrative is false or, more commonly—as with Sotomayor's dissent in *Strieff*—a cover-up of a truer narrative, one that may lead to future nightmare. The facts on the ground may not be malleable, but that doesn't mean that the stories that must be told about them if they are to be intelligible are not protean, as shape-shifting as our diverse ways of imagining and understanding the world. They depend on what seems to you a well-formed narrative that produces conviction.

Constitutional Narratives and the American Covenant

Any society needs myths of origin to confer meaning on itself—meaning that may appear sacred. As I suggested in chapter 1, such myths can be dangerous—they probably have been more noxious than beneficial over history—and need to be seen for what they are: constructed fictions, not revealed truths. They are narratives of origin "explaining" how we got to be the way we are. Americans regularly call on many such narratives, and one of the most curious is the story of the US Constitution—curious, because it is not obvious why any society should need such technical and complex narratives as those of constitutional law to make sense of itself. Yet since the American Constitution in many ways takes the place of the foundational events, myths, and rulers held sacred in other societies, the continuing need to find meaning in the narratives spun from it may not be so surprising. Still, our unabated reverence for and obedience to these narratives, even when they seem counterintuitive and socially unproductive, demand some thinking about.

A few decades ago, Justice William Brennan, dissenting in the Supreme Court case *Michael H. v. Gerald D.*, declared of Justice Antonin Scalia's plurality opinion: "The document that the plurality construes today is unfamiliar to me. It is not the living charter that I have taken to be our Constitution; it is instead a stagnant, archaic, hidebound document steeped in the prejudices and superstitions of a time long past."[11] Since Brennan wrote those words, "originalism" in constitutional jurisprudence seems to have won the day, even among its opponents. That "living charter" seems to be evoked less frequently, and the "prejudices and superstitions of a time long past" appear to command ever greater allegiance on the Court. In *District of Columbia v. Heller*, for instance—the 2008 case that held that the Second Amendment guarantees an individual right to bear arms—both Scalia's majority opinion and the lead dissent by Justice John Paul Stevens stake their claims on how that amendment should be understood in its original historical context.[12] That is, both Stevens and Scalia appear to sign on to what Scalia long argued should be the underlying principle of constitutional interpretation: fidelity to the "original understanding" of the document, as evinced by the ratification debates, discussions in *The Federalist*, and similar writings. *Heller* led a number of commentators to declare that we have all become originalists.[13] This is not entirely true—originalism is still subject to much criticism—but it is undeniable that debates about the origins of our laws, our ideologies, and our social commitments matter very much in contemporary America. Strange that this should be so in a country that has always seen itself as resolutely turned to the future. But perhaps that future orientation inevitably calls for attention to the past, and to the narrative of how we got from past to present.

In principle, "originalists" would discard precedent in favor of abiding by the words of the Constitution; yet the common law tradition that the United States shares with Britain usually derives current legal decisions from precedent, fitting the present case to analogous cases that have come before. In constitutional adjudication, the precedents derive from and lead back to the written document that is considered the supreme law of the land while most often taking account of the interpretive history built upon it. Respect for precedent is enshrined in the doctrine of *stare decisis*: the rule that one does not change the decisions made in the past but builds upon them. One of the best expositions of what this means and how it works comes from Justices Sandra Day O'Connor, David Souter, and Anthony Kennedy, authors of the "joint opinion" in *Planned Parenthood of Southeastern Pennsylvania v. Casey*, the 1992 case that reaffirmed (with some modifications) the right to abortion first secured in *Roe v. Wade* (1973).[14] It's an effort to explain why it is that even if the court would not rule as it did in *Roe* if the case were coming to it afresh, it is important to reaffirm its ruling close to a generation later. Beyond that, it is an effort to explain the source of the court's authority to write the constitutional narrative.

The very concept of the rule of law, write O'Connor, Souter, and Kennedy, requires continuity over time so that citizens may rely upon the law. Thus, though one might rule differently were the issue at hand coming to adjudication for the first time, the fact that it was once ruled upon in a certain way, and that people have come to rely on that ruling, alters the second adjudication, giving a heavy burden of proof to those who would reverse course. As the joint opinion puts it, to both those who approve and those who disapprove but struggle to respect a constitutional ruling, "the Court implicitly undertakes to remain steadfast." "Steadfastness" is indeed not only pragmatic—assuring a uniform law that can be relied upon—but also moral: "Like the character of an individual, the legitimacy of the Court must be earned over time." Note that "over time": earned legitimacy depends on a history, a narrative of consistency.[15] The moral court, like the moral individual, must be true to itself.

There are times when the court can and must overrule itself: the joint opinion points to the overturning of the laissez-fare economics of *Lochner v. New York* (1905) by *West Coast Hotel Company v. Parrish* (1937), and—the most famous reversal—*Plessy v. Ferguson* (1896) overruled by *Brown v. Board of Education of Topeka* (1954): two striking rejections of *stare decisis* which the court here describes as "applications of constitutional principle to facts as they had not been seen by the Court before." Such reversals must be rare if the court is to maintain its moral authority to speak in ways that will be accepted and complied with. As the joint opinion explains:

> The Court must take care to speak and act in ways that allow people to accept its decisions on the terms the Court claims for them, as grounded truly in principle, not as compromises with social and political pressures having, as such, no bearing on the principled choices that the Court is obliged to make. Thus, the Court's legitimacy depends on making legally principled decisions under circumstances in which their principled character is sufficiently plausible to be accepted by the Nation.

Sequence and consequence in the constitutional narrative must not be random; the new must be logically entailed by precedent. The most apt words in the lines quoted may be "sufficiently plausible," a phrase that alerts us to the rhetoric deployed by the court. What is "sufficiently plausible" is that which persuades its readership, its audiences, which is to say a narrative that convinces. "Sufficiently plausible" is tautological—but in a way that any public argument must be: it judges the effectiveness of persuasion by its capacity to persuade in fact. The logic of the joint opinion is necessarily circular: it claims that rulings by the court will be accepted if and when they appear to fit seamlessly with the master narrative, which in turn means that their acceptance creates a seamless narrative, the perception that the law is "steadfast." What "suffices" for the "sufficiently plausible" is . . . what suffices. In conclusion to its discussion of *stare decisis,* the joint opinion raises the moral stakes:

> Our Constitution is a covenant running from the first generation of Americans to us and then to future generations. It is a coherent succession. Each generation must learn anew that the Constitution's written terms embody ideas and aspirations that must survive more ages than one. We accept our responsibility not to retreat from interpreting the full meaning of the covenant in light of all of our precedents. We invoke it once again to define the freedom guaranteed by the Constitution's own promise, the promise of liberty.

Here the court presents itself as the author of covenantal narratives, stories that establish and maintain a sacred bond between generations of Americans, so that the present and future exist as realizations of that which lay latent within the past. Laws must preserve the "promise of liberty" as the realization of a prophecy, as fulfillment of the covenant.

The court's logic here is to a large degree the logic of narrative itself. It offers an example of what the narrative theorist Gérard Genette calls the "determination of means by ends ... of causes by effects." Genette writes:

> This is that paradoxical logic of fiction which requires us to define every element, every unit of the narrative by its functional character, that is to say among other things by its correlation with another unit, and to account for the first (in the order of narrative temporality) by the second, and so on—from which it follows that the last [unit] is the one that governs all the others, and that is itself governed by nothing.[16]

Earlier events or actions make sense only as their meaning becomes clear through subsequent events, in what Genette calls a "paradoxical logic." Or, as Roland Barthes suggests, narrative is built on a generalization of the philosophical error of *post hoc, ergo propter hoc*: narrative plotting makes it seem that if B follows A it is because B is logically entailed by A, whereas in fact A becomes causal only in terms of B.[17] In law, this narrative logic may to some degree cover over a tension between what is called for in order to create the seamless plot and the other paths—other claims to justice—that were not taken.

The eloquent defense of *stare decisis* in *Planned Parenthood v. Casey* suggests that the narrative of constitutional interpretation depends on the retrospective interpretation of the prior narrative in light of the new episode the court is adding to it. This must be the case, since dissenters can and do argue that the new decision precisely misinterprets prior history, which would be better served—given a more plausible plot line—by a different ruling (see Alito's and Kagan's opinions in *Jardines*, for instance). The form taken by all constitutional interpretation follows this model: that the proposed interpretation realizes the true meaning of the constitutional narrative better than the alternatives. It provides the better ending, defined in terms of the ending that makes better sense of the plot leading up to it.

It falls within this same logic that constitutional narratives, whether written by originalists or not, often claim they are based on a return to the beginning—to the text and context of the Constitution itself—in order to track forward the development of text and interpretation. This is especially true when the court is aware it is propounding what will appear to be a radically new interpretation, one that won't be accepted without resistance. Thus, in the landmark case *Miranda v. Arizona* (1966)—which extended the Fifth Amendment protection against self-incrimination to police interrogation of criminal suspects—Chief Justice Earl Warren claims: "The cases before us raise questions which go to the roots of our concepts of American criminal jurisprudence."[18] And also: "We start here . . . with the premise that our holding is not an innovation in our jurisprudence, but is an application of principles long recognized" and an "explication of basic rights that are enshrined in our Constitution. . . . These precious rights were fixed in our Constitution only after centuries of persecution and struggle." Warren argues that the ruling in *Miranda* is simply the emergence into the light of day of what was all along entailed by the Fifth Amendment privilege against self-incrimination. It's as if the history of constitutional law had always contained within itself the seed that now matures into Miranda doctrine.

Inevitably, the dissenters in *Miranda* claim that Warren has the story wrong. To Warren's assertion that the majority's ruling is "not an innovation," Justice Byron White ripostes that "the Court has not discovered or found the law...what it has done is to make new law." Another dissent, by Justice John Marshall Harlan, refers to the court's "new constitutional code of rules for confessions." Harlan sets out to mark the point at which the court "jumped the rails"—the point at which it deviated, with dire results, from the correct narrative line. He, too, reaches back to origins to claim that the majority's reliance on the Fifth Amendment is a "trompe l'oeil," a deceptive reality effect that it has taken for reality itself. Harlan brands the majority's ruling as a wholly implausible narrative: "One is entitled to feel astonished that the Constitution can be read to produce this result." And in his peroration, Harlan declares, citing the words of a bygone justice, Robert Jackson: "This Court is forever adding new stories to the temples of constitutional law, and the temples have a way of collapsing when one story too many is added." There seems to be an interesting pun here, on stories as features of houses and stories as narrative. In both senses of the word "story" Harlan implies that the new narrative episode written in *Miranda* brings the collapse of the whole narrative. It makes it the wrong story.

For all their discourse of origins, then, both majority and dissent in *Miranda* accept the notion that the outcome of the story, the ending written (however provisionally) by the current ruling, determines the meaning of the story's earlier episodes: the present rewrites the past.[19] They discover here—though without explicit awareness—the retrospective logic of narrative. Narrative begins from the end, which confers meaning on beginning and middle, which indeed allows us to understand what can be identified as beginning and middle. When we read a narrative, we read toward the end, not in knowledge of what it will bring but in anticipation that it will bring retrospective illumination to the plot leading to it. Similarly, Sartre's fictional spokesman Roquentin in *Nausea* argues that when you tell a story—as opposed to living it—you only appear to begin at the beginning, since the knowledge that an end lies ahead confers intention and meaning on the actions recounted. The novelistic hero lives life backwards from the end, all his actions seen as "annunciations" of the future outcome. It is in the peculiar nature of narrative as a sense-making system that clues are revealing, that prior events are prior, and causes are causal only retrospectively, in a reading back from the end.

We come back to Carlo Ginzburg's speculation that narrative originated in a society of hunters, in the tracing of signs pointing to the passage of quarry. Learning to put those clues together in a narrative chain that would lead to the quarry offers a form of reasoning that is properly speaking neither deductive nor inductive but precisely narrative: the creation of meaningful sequences. Ginzburg compares this huntsman's paradigm to ancient Mesopotamian law, which worked through discussions of concrete examples rather than the collection of statutes—much like Anglo-American "case law"—and to Mesopotamian divination, based on the minute investigation of seemingly trivial details: "animals' innards, drops of oil on the water, stars, involuntary movements of the body."[20] The same paradigm is found in the divinatory and jurisprudential texts, with this difference: that the former are directed to the future, the latter to the past. Generalizing further, Ginzburg suggests that all narrative modes of knowing (such as archaeology, paleontology, geology) make what he calls "retrospective prophecies": prophecies that work backwards from outcome to that which announces and calls for the outcome.

The notion of retrospective prophecy perfectly characterizes the constitutional narratives written by the Supreme Court, and perhaps indeed most legal narrative: the ruling in the case at hand exists as the fulfillment of what was called for in the beginning—much as early Christian theologians argued that the Gospels offered a realization of the prophetic narratives of the Hebrew Bible, as figure and fulfillment. For Augustine, for instance, Moses is a *figura Christi*, prefiguring Christ; Noah's Ark a *praefiguratio ecclesiae*, figure of the future Church.[21] It is as if the past were pregnant with the present, waiting to be delivered of the wisdom which the court reveals in its ruling. Recall *Casey*'s use of the word "covenant" to describe the Constitution, precisely in its historical relation to the citizenry. Each new ruling by the Supreme Court is an episode in the unfolding narrative of that covenant.

The argument from origins that you get in a case such as *Miranda* is doubtless sincere as well as strategic in its desire to make origins entail a certain outcome, to argue: this is not an innovation in our jurisprudence but the present application of long-standing principle and precedent, part of that "coherent succession." Nonetheless, we can recognize in it the structure of the retrospective prophecy in its arguing that the stipulated outcome is the only way to realize the history of constitutional interpretation, to deliver on its immanent meaning. Narrative always has Genette's "double logic," telling its story from the beginning but structuring it in terms of an end that makes sense of that beginning. It is like the structure of trauma in many of Freud's case histories, where a later event will retrospectively sexualize and thus confer traumatic force on an earlier event.

Judicial opinions are full of a rhetoric of constraint: judges cannot rule otherwise than they are doing because they are constrained by precedent. Whatever their personal preferences in the case, the outcome is imposed upon them by the history leading up to it. Furthermore, it often seems that the more the court's ruling might be interpreted as an innovation—a break with the past—the more the rhetoric of the opinion asserts the seamless continuity of its ruling with the past, its simple and necessary entailment.[22] The rhetoric of *stare decisis* may in this manner be something of a cover-up, a claim that the weight of the past narrative dictates this outcome— whereas the dissent, as in *Miranda*, will claim that the court has "jumped the rails," lost the proper design and intention of the narrative, given the wrong plot, betrayed the "covenant." To say this is not to argue that the narrative traced from origin to endpoint is useless or false. The conclusion to the narrative will be acceptable to its audiences only if the construction of the narrative has been "sufficiently plausible," to use the words of *Casey* again. As Dr. Watson says to Sherlock Holmes at the end of one of their cases, "'You reasoned it out beautifully,' I exclaimed in unfeigned admiration. 'It is so long a chain, and yet every link rings true.'"[23] The chain composed of true links is perspicuous as a chain only at the end. The detective story is in this an exemplary form of narrative because it shows so well how this chain is constructed.

"*It is so ordered*": the court has managed to make its orders, its outcomes, stick with remarkable consistency. Presidents, legislators, police, citizens accept the order however much they may disagree with it, however fervent their protests may be. Even such a paltry and embarrassing decision as *Bush v. Gore*—devoid of legal reasoning, patently jury-rigged for the occasion—in 2000 managed to make itself obeyed. There are a very few moments in American history when the court's narrative has seemed so implausible and so unacceptable to parts of the country that the issue has created civil unrest. The most notable was no doubt *Dred Scott v. Sanford* (1857), which provided a decision so contentious and unsatisfactory—and a narrative of American citizenship so starkly exclusionary—that its issues could be decided only by Civil War. Closer to our own time, the court's decisions in *Brown v. Board of Education*, I and II (1954 and 1955), provoked various degrees of resistance, most notably and violently the refusal of Governor Orval Faubus of Arkansas to execute the court's orders. Faubus instead used the power of the executive for the law's infraction, refusing entry by African American students to Little Rock Central High School and mobilizing the Arkansas National Guard to bar the doors. This was followed by President Dwight Eisenhower's sending units of the 101st Airborne Division to Little Rock to force the students' entry.

This crisis in resistance to the court's order—unprecedented in US history—spurred the court to assemble in special session, in September 1958, and to issue its ruling in *Cooper v. Aaron*, affirming the Eighth Circuit Court of Appeals's reversal of the Arkansas District Court's grant of a stay of integration in Little Rock.[24] *Cooper v. Aaron* has the distinction of offering not simply the unanimous opinion of the court but, as well, the names of all nine justices spelled out at the outset of the opinion. Here the court reaches back to the very genesis of its power of judicial review in *Marbury v. Madison*:

In 1803, Chief Justice Marshall, speaking for a unanimous Court, referring to the Constitution as "the fundamental and paramount law of the nation," declared in the notable case of *Marbury v. Madison*, 1 Cranch 137, 177, that "It is emphatically the province and duty of the judicial department to say what the law is." This decision declared the basic principle that the federal judiciary is supreme in the exposition of the law of the Constitution, and that principle has ever since been respected by this Court and the Country as a permanent and indispensable feature of our constitutional system. It follows that the interpretation of the Fourteenth Amendment enunciated by this Court in the *Brown* case is the supreme law of the land.

Like the giant Antaeus touching ground to regain strength, the court here touches its very beginnings as a branch of American governmental power. Note "it follows that": not only the Constitution but the interpretive narratives spun from it are the supreme law.

Appended to the unanimous opinion in *Cooper v. Aaron* is a concurring opinion by Justice Felix Frankfurter—a narcissistic move on his part that somewhat disfigures the impressive unity of the court's self-presentation in the case, but a document that is full of interest. It is a tense, eloquent, strained piece of judicial rhetoric in reaction to the "profoundly subversive" use of state executive power to thwart rather than carry out the law, and a reaffirmation of "this Court's adamant decisions in the Brown case"—decisions, the adjective implies, set in stone. Frankfurter reaches back even further than *Marbury v. Madison* to quote John Adams on the need for a "government of Laws, not of Men." Frankfurter goes on to cite from his own concurring opinion in *United States v. United Mine Workers*:[25]

148

The conception of a government by laws dominated the thoughts of those who founded this Nation and designed its Constitution, although they knew as well as the belittlers of the conception that laws have to be made, interpreted and enforced by men. To that end, they set apart a body of men, who were to be the depositories of law, who, by their disciplined training and character and by withdrawal from the usual temptations of private interest, may reasonably be expected to be "as free, impartial, and independent as the lot of humanity will admit." So strongly were the framers of the Constitution bent on securing a reign of law that they endowed the judicial office with extraordinary safeguards and prestige.

Here the priestly caste of the Supreme Court Justices emerges from the shadows to stand in full view. These interpreters are not like any others. They are "depositories of law." They are set aside in the temple to contemplate and to expound the law—which here sounds very much like the Law. Frankfurter has sensed that a subversive threat of disobedience to the constitutional narrative declared by the court needs to be met with a rhetoric that at the last foregrounds the very status of the court itself, the solemn context of its speech acts.

"It is so ordered": the outcome so proposed writes the past history of interpretation in a rhetoric that both touches back to origins and foregrounds its own constraints in reaching this end. The court offers an arche-teleological discourse that stresses origin and constraint in order to achieve ends. Such a narrative of the covenant is no doubt simply necessary—covenantal discourse, one might say, is like that. The structure of prophecy and fulfillment may be a requirement of any master narrative that governs societies. If the

discourse of American constitutional interpretation turns out to be remarkably biblical, that should not come as a surprise, since it is difficult to imagine a society without some sort of providential discourse underlying it. If the Constitution is our myth of origins, we must expect it to generate mythic narrative consequences. But it should no doubt be subjected to a more acute awareness of its narrative logic.

And yet, claims for the importance of story within the law put forth in legal scholarship have often seemed to me to go in a direction that reinforces the prejudices against bringing analytic attention to legal narrative. "Storytelling for Oppositionists and Others," an essay by the law professor Richard Delgado in a 1989 issue of *Michigan Law Review*, inaugurated a notion that narrative offers a tool to those traditionally deprived of standing in the law to make their grievances heard. Narrative stands in opposition to standard legal discourse; it is radical, unsettling, and largely ethical and emotional in its claims. Certainly there is truth this view, and many an essay since has developed its implications, especially in the use of real-life narratives that contest standard legal discourse.[26] But the storytelling for oppositionists and out-groups movement had the effect of identifying story too narrowly, and assigning it a wholly positive value. In the process it deflected attention from the permeation of the law in every aspect with story, and from the fact that stories can serve the worse as well as the better cause. There is nothing inherently worthy or unworthy about narrative—it's the uses it is put to that count. And conferring a particular moral valence on story tends to push away what is needed: analytic attention to the role narrative inevitably plays in the law.

So I find myself more or less constrained to end this discussion with a boring plea: Let legal actors learn something about narrative, and some of the analytic tools for studying narrative that go under the head of "narratology." The languages of the law tend to be hermetic, resistant to change, especially when it comes from without the profession. But it seems to me that there is by now sufficient evidence that storytelling plays a huge part in the law for law school curricula, for instance, to include study of it. Attention to storytelling does in fact have a place in legal teaching, but it's generally relegated to the margins: to clinical courses on trial and advocacy that are neither central to the curriculum nor accorded prestige. Law may continue its practical engagements with narrative without any analytic consciousness of its practices. Which makes it all the more important that those outside the law continue to insist that it is narratively constructed, and that its stories need to be seen for what they are and subjected to our suspicious attention.

Talking about stories in the law lets us begin to understand how the analytic study of narrative can extend well beyond its place of origin, in literary studies. "Narratology" should indeed be a powerful export from literary to the many other kinds of study that beg for narrative analysis. This enterprise has begun—the work of narrative, as I noted in my first chapter, has been registered in history, philosophy, economics, medicine, and other fields, though its constitutive role differs in various fields and is often only marginally accepted as important. Still, it's clear that narrative dominates in much of contemporary reality, in the media, in corporations, in politics, and that the task of narrative analysis is far from finished. We've only begun to shine analytic light on how stories are used to motivate and control populations. The weight of the unanalyzed stories, those that are propagated and accepted as true and necessary myths, may kill us yet.

We live at a time when knowledge generated by the humanities in general and literary study in particular is often publicly devalued, or even derided. The only knowledge worth having is thought to be instrumental: that which gives you direct leverage on the world. The critique provided by the tools of literary analysis is more oblique but I think no less important. I would argue that we need, more than ever, the reflective knowledge that the humanities can provide, very much including analysis of the dominant stories of our economies, our ethics, our politics. The role of the literary humanities in public life may be this: to provide public tools of resistance to bogus and totalizing world explanations, to broadcast the means to dismantle the noxious myths of our time.

Acknowledgments

THE THINKING IN THIS BOOK goes way back, to my early teaching and writing, and in the process represents more debts to students, colleagues, friends than I can easily acknowledge. Let me mention in particular David Marshall, Eric Bulson, Martin Stone, Paul Gewirtz, Robert Post, and Brigid Doherty as classroom collaborators from whom I learned much; and the late Michael Holquist and Alvin Kernan. Also Rachel Bowlby, D. A. Miller, David Shields, Anthony Amsterdam, Robert Ferguson, Philip Meyer, Robin West, Paolo Tortonese, Elaine Scarry, David Bordwell, and Maureen Chun. Some of the material in chapter 3 is adapted from piece published in *The New York Review of Books*; in chapter 5 from an essay published in *Romanic Review*; and in chapter 6 from essays published in *Daedalus* and *PMLA*. A first trial of some of my ideas appeared in *The Chronicle of Higher Education*. I thank the publications and the editors who asked me to contribute: Michael Shae, Elisabeth Ladenson, Denis Donoghue, and Chenxi Tang. And thanks to Heidi Downey for her sensitive and skillful copyediting. Thanks finally to Edwin Frank and Sara Kramer, who have made New York Review Books such a remarkable place to publish.

Notes

STORIES ABOUNDING: THE WORLD OVERTAKEN BY
NARRATIVE

1. Jerome Bruner, "The Narrative Construction of Reality," in *Critical Inquiry* 18, no. 1 (1991): 1–21. Further information about the study of narrative can be found in the first chapter of my *Reading for the Plot: Design and Intention in Narrative* (1984; Cambridge: Harvard University Press, 1992).

2. A pale reflection of what we were up to in the course can be found in the textbook anthology compiled by Alvin B. Kernan, J. Michael Holquist, and myself, titled (in pre-gender neutral language) *Man and His Fictions: An Introduction to Fiction-Making, Its Forms and Uses* (New York: Harcourt Brace Jovanovich, 1973). The anthology was never used in the course, however, and adopted at very few other institutions.

3. Roland Barthes, "Introduction à l'analyse structurale des récits," *Communications* 8 (1966). English trans. Richard Howard, "Introduction to the Structural Analysis of Narratives," in *A Barthes Reader*, ed. Susan Sontag (New York: Hill & Wang, 1982). My translation.

4. Jean-François Lyotard, *La Condition postmoderne* (Paris: Éditions de Minuit, 1979); English trans. Geoffrey Bennington and Brian Massumi, *The Postmodern Condition* (Minneapolis: University of Minnesota Press, 1984).

5. Ben Smith, "Arrest in Canada Casts a Shadow on a New York Times Star, and the Times," *New York Times*, October 12, 2020.

6. Christian Salmon, *Storytelling: La Machine à fabriquer des histoires et formatter les esprits* (Paris: La Découverte, 2007); English trans. David Macey,

Storytelling: Bewitching the Modern Mind (London: Verso, 2010). The subtitle of the English translation gives a hint that it is somewhat different in emphasis than the French original. Salmon mentions as an inspiration for his book an essay of mine: "Stories Abounding," *Chronicle of Higher Education*, March 23, 2001.

7. "Let's Talk About Higher Wages," *New York Times*, November 29, 2020.

8. Annette Simmons, *Whoever Tells the Best Story Wins* (New York: AMACOM, 2007), 211. See also Lisa Cron, *Story or Die: How to Use Brain Science to Engage, Persuade, and Change Minds in Business and in Life* (California and New York: Ten Speed, 2021).

9. See https://storycorps.org.

10. Story Skills Workshop: https://akimbo.com/thepodcastingworkshop.

11. On Reagan's confusions of fact and film, see Gary Wills, *Reagan's America: Innocents at Home* (New York: Doubleday, 1986).

12. Louis O. Mink, "Narrative Form as a Cognitive Instrument," in Mink, *Historical Understanding*, ed. Brian Fay, Eugene O. Golob, and Richard T. Vann (Ithaca: Cornell University Press, 1987), 201.

13. Anthony G. Amsterdam and Jerome Bruner, *Minding the Law* (Cambridge: Harvard University Press, 2000), 111.

14. For an example of this standard viewpoint, see Richard Posner reviewing Peter Brooks and Paul Gewirtz, *Law's Stories: Narrative and Rhetoric in the Law* in "Legal Narratology," *University of Chicago Law Review* 64 (1997): 737.

15. See Hanna Meretoja, "Narrative and Human Existence: Ontology, Epistemology, and Ethics," *New Literary History* 45, no. 1 (2014).

16. The bibliography of works by and about the Russian Formalists is extensive; for a succinct account of the group, see Peter Steiner, "Russian Formalism," in *The Cambridge History of Literary Criticism*, ed. Raman Selden (Cambridge: Cambridge University Press, 1995), 8:11–30.

17. See Barthes, "Introduction à l'analyse structurale des récits"; Sontag, *Barthes Reader*. See Gérard Genette, *Discours du récit* in *Figures III* (Paris: Éditions du Seuil, 1972). English trans. Jane Lewin, *Narrative Discourse: An Essay in Method* (Ithaca: Cornell University Press, 1983). For those interested in systematic study of narrative, in addition to the works cited I recommend Shlomith Rimmon-Kenan, *Narrative Fiction: Contemporary*

Poetics (London: Methuen, 1983), and H. Porter Abbott, *The Cambridge Introduction to Narrative* (Cambridge: Cambridge University Press, 2002).

18. Carlo Ginzburg, "Spie. Radici di un paradigma indizario," in *Miti, emblemi, spie: Morfologia e storia* (Turin: Einaudi, 1986), 166. English trans. John and Anne C. Tedeschi, "Clues: Roots of an Evidential Paradigm," in *Myths, Emblems, and the Historical Method* (Baltimore: Johns Hopkins University Press, 1990), 102. In my quotes from Ginzburg's essay I have modified the Tedeschi translation in places to give a more literal rendition. Ginzburg's insights underlie the major study by Terence Cave, *Recognitions: A Study in Poetics* (Oxford: Clarendon, 1988).

19. On Darwin and the novel, see Gillian Beer, *Darwin's Plots: Evolutionary Narrative in Darwin, George Eliot and Nineteenth-Century Fiction* (London: Routledge and Kegan Paul, 1983), and George Levine, *Darwin and the Novelists: Patterns of Science in Victorian Fiction* (Cambridge: Harvard University Press, 1988). I think one could argue that the dominant figures of modern culture, from the nineteenth into the twentieth century—that is to say, Darwin, Marx, and Freud—all see explanation as inherently narrative.

20. See Roman Jakobson, "Two Aspects of Language and Two Types of Aphasic Disturbances," in Jakobson and Morris Halle, *Fundamentals of Language* (The Hague: Mouton, 1956).

21. Galen Strawson, "A Fallacy of Our Age," in *Things That Bother Me: Death, Freedom, the Self, Etc.* (New York: New York Review Books, 2018), 45.

22. Strawson, *Things That Bother Me*, 55, citing Charles Taylor, *Sources of the Self: Making of the Modern Identity* (Cambridge: Harvard University Press, 1989), 47, 52.

23. Strawson, *Things That Bother Me*, 56, citing Alasdair MacIntyre, *After Virtue: A Study in Moral Theory* (London: Duckworth, 1981), 203–4.

24. Strawson, *Things That Bother Me*, 58. See Walter Benjamin, "The Storyteller," in *The Storyteller Essays*, ed. Samuel Titan, trans. Tess Lewis (New York: New York Review Books, 2019)

25. See my chapter "Fictions of the Wolf Man: Freud and Narrative Understanding," in *Reading for the Plot*, 264–85, and also my *Psychoanalysis and Storytelling* (Oxford: Blackwell, 1994).

26. Strawson, *Things That Bother Me*, 178.

27. Jorge Luis Borges, "Tlön, Uqbar, Orbis Tertius," trans. James E. Irby, in *Labyrinths: Selected Stories and Other Writings* (Norfolk, CT: New Directions, 1962), 15–16.

28. On fictions and myths, see Frank Kermode, *The Sense of an Ending: Studies in the Theory of Fiction* (New York: Oxford University Press, 1967), a book that has long been important in my own thinking about narrative.

29. On the *Enola Gay* controversy, as well as many other issues in the representation of the past, see Sarah Maza, *Thinking About History* (Chicago: University of Chicago Press, 2017).

30. Ezra Klein, "What's Really Behind the 1619 Backlash? An Interview with Nikole Hannah-Jones and Ta-Nehisi Coates," *New York Times*, July 30, 2021.

31. Jake Silverstein, "Why We Published the 1619 Project," *New York Times Magazine*, December 10, 2019.

THE EPISTEMOLOGY OF NARRATIVE; OR, HOW CAN THE TELLER KNOW THE TALE?

1. Psycho-narration, quoted monologue, and narrated monologue are Dorrit Cohn's useful terms; narrated monologue corresponds to what the French call *style indirect libre*, which seems to me the most important technique for rendering consciousness in the modern novel. See Cohn, *Transparent Minds: Narrative Modes for Presenting Consciousness in Fiction* (Princeton: Princeton University Press, 1984). I thank Rachel Bowlby for her reading of and generous comments on this chapter (though she does not agree with my critique of *The Girl on the Train*).

2. "Theory of mind" as an activity triggered in reading novels has become an important concept in criticism inspired by cognitive neuroscience. See, among other examples, Lisa Zunshine, *Why We Read Fiction: Theory of Mind and the Novel* (Columbus: Ohio State University Press, 2006); Blakey Vermeule, *Why Do We Care About Literary Characters?* (Baltimore: Johns Hopkins University Press, 2009); and Jonathan Kramnick, *Paper Minds: Literature and the Ecology of Consciousness* (Chicago: University of Chicago Press, 2018).

3. See on this question Ruediger Heinze, "Violations of Mimetic Epistemology in First-Person Narrative Fiction," *Narrative* 16, no. 3 (2008): 279–97.

4. Paula Hawkins, *The Girl on the Train* (New York: Riverhead, 2015), 304.

5. Rimmon-Kenan, *Narrative Fiction*, 80.

6. See Dorrit Cohn on first-person present-tense narratives, which, she says, offer "absolutely unreal narrative situations, enabling characters to live and tell—and even to die and tell—simultaneously." Cohn, *The Distinction of Fiction* (Baltimore: Johns Hopkins University Press, 1999), 33.

7. Leo Tolstoy, *The Death of Ivan Ilyich and Other Stories*, trans. Richard Pevear and Larissa Volokhonsky (New York: Knopf, 2009), 91.

8. Gustave Flaubert, *Un Coeur simple*, in *Trois Contes* (Paris: Garnier/Flammarion, 1986), 78. My translation.

9. See James Wood, "The Blue River of Truth," *New Republic*, August 1, 2005.

10. "J'ai trouvé les moyens, avec beaucoup de soin et de peine, de recouvrer une copie correcte de la traduction de cinq Lettres Portugaises qui ont été écrites à un gentilhomme de qualité qui servoit en Portugal." Gabriel de Guilleragues, *Lettres portugaises*, ed. Frédéric Deloffre (Paris: Garnier, 1962).

11. Frédéric Deloffre, cited by Vivienne G. Mylne in *The Eighteenth-Century French Novel: Techniques of Illusion* (Manchester: Manchester University Press, 1965), 145.

12. Denis Diderot, *Éloge de Richardson*, in *Oeuvres esthétiques*, ed. Paul Vernière (Paris: Garnier, 2001).

13. Samuel Richardson, letter of April 9, 1748, in Alan Dugald McKillop, *The Early Masters of English Fiction* (Lawrence: University of Kansas Press, 1956), 42.

14. Daniel Defoe, *The Fortunes and Misfortunes of the Famous Moll Flanders* (London: Penguin, 1989), 37.

15. On censorship of novels in the French eighteenth century, see Georges May, *Le Dilemme du roman français au XVIIIe siècle* (New Haven: Yale University Press, 1963).

16. On the notion of paratext, see Gérard Genette, *Seuils* (Paris: Éditions du Seuil, 1987); English trans. Jane Lewin, *Paratexts: Thresholds of Interpretation* (Cambridge: Cambridge University Press, 1997)

17. I discuss "The Musgrave Ritual" in my *Reading for the Plot*, 23–27.

18. Arthur Conan Doyle, "The Naval Treaty," in Conan Doyle, *Sherlock Holmes: The Complete Novels and Stories* (New York: Bantam Classics, 2003), 1:734.

19. Henry James, Preface to *The Golden Bowl*, in *Henry James: Literary Criticism* (New York: Library of America, 1984), 2:1322.

20. William Faulkner, *Absalom, Absalom!* (1936; New York: Vintage, 1990), 283. Other quotations in this discussion: 214, 220.

21. Cleanth Brooks argues that Quentin must have learned this information in an unrecorded conversation with Henry Sutpen during that visit to Sutpen's Hundred in 1910—an ingenious but possibly unjustified speculation since the needed clue is there, as it were, in plain view, but missed by that eminent scholar of Faulkner. Brooks, *William Faulkner: The Yoknapatawpha Country* (New Haven: Yale University Press, 1963), 314–17, 436–41. See also Michael Gorra, *The Saddest Words: William Faulkner's Civil War* (New York: Norton, 2020). Gorra does not come to a decision on the source of Quentin's knowledge.

22. Sigmund Freud, "Constructions in Analysis," in *The Standard Edition of the Complete Psychological Works* (London: Hogarth, 1953–74), 23:265–66.

23. On this topic, see Ann Gaylin, *Eavesdropping in the Novel from Austen to Proust* (Cambridge: Cambridge University Press, 2002).

24. Hayden White, *The Content of the Form: Narrative Discourse and Historical Representation* (Baltimore: Johns Hopkins University Press, 1987), 215n.

THE TELLER, THE TOLD, THE DIFFERENCE IT MAKES

1. See William Labov and Joshua Waletzky, "Narrative Analysis: Oral Versions of Personal Experience," in *Essays on the Verbal and Visual Arts*, ed. June Helm (Seattle: University of Washington Press, 1967). I say "he" here because all the speakers recorded were male.

2. Socrates says of speeches: "And when they have been once written down they are tumbled about anywhere among those who may or may not understand them, and know not to whom they should reply, to whom not: and, if they are maltreated or abused, they have no parent to protect them; and they cannot protect or defend themselves." Plato, *Phaedrus*, 275e, trans. Benjamin Jowett, in *The Collected Dialogues*, ed. Edith Hamilton and Huntington Cairns (Princeton: Princeton Univeristy Press,1963), 521. I take this point from Charles Larmore, "The Ethics of Reading," in *The Humanities and Public Life*, ed. Peter Brooks with Hilary Jewett (New York: Fordham University Press, 2014).

3. John D. Niles, *Homo Narrans: The Poetics and Anthropology of Oral Literature* (Philadelphia: University of Pennsylvania Press, 2010), 53.

4. "Translator's Preface," in *The Book of the Thousand Nights and a Night*, trans. Richard Burton (Benares: Kamashastra Society, 1885), 8.

5. Georg Lukács, "*Illusions Perdues*," trans. Paul Laveau, in *Balzac et le réalisme français* (Paris: F. Maspéro, 1969).

6. *Another Study of Womankind*, trans. Jordan Stump, in Honoré de Balzac, *The Human Comedy: Selected Stories*, ed. Peter Brooks (New York: New York Review Books, 2014), 18. *Autre Étude de femme*, in Honoré de Balzac, *La Comédie humaine*, 12 vols. (Paris: Bibliothèque de la Pléiade, 1976), 3:674.

7. William Labov, "Some Further Steps in Narrative Analysis," *Journal of Narrative and Life History* 7, nos. 1–4 (1997): 395.

8. Guy de Maupassant, "Une Ruse," in *Contes et nouvelles*, ed. Louis Forestier (Paris: Bibliothèque de la Pléiade, 1974). Often translated into English as "An Artifice."

9. Saki (H. H. Munro), "The Open Window," in *Beasts and Super-Beasts* (London: John Lane, 1914).

10. Joseph Conrad, *Heart of Darkness*, ed. Owen Knowles and Allan H. Simmons (Cambridge: Cambridge University Press, 2018), 83.

11. On this final "pensivity" of the tale, see Roland Barthes, *S/Z*, trans. Richard Miller (New York: Hill & Wang, 1974); in French: *S/Z* (Paris: Éditions du Seuil, 1970).

12. Charlotte Brontë, *Villette* (1853; London: Penguin, 2004), 341. Other quotations in this discussion: 364, 380, 73, 77, 80–81, 178, 180, 200, 245.

13. Walter Benjamin, "The Storyteller," in *The Storyteller Essays*, ed. Samuel Titan, trans. Tess Lewis (New York: New York Review Books, 2019), 56. Other quotations in this discussion: 49, 59, 87, 91, 65–66, 51–52, 9, 41.

14. See my essay "Dying Declarations," in *Fictional Discourse and the Law*, ed. Hans J. Lind (Abingdon: Routledge, 2020), 117–23.

15. See my discussion of these accounts in *Troubling Confessions: Speaking Guilt in Law and Literature* (Chicago: University of Chicago Press, 2000), 159–60.

16. See the dissent registered by Daniel Defoe's Moll Flanders: "The ordinary of Newgate came to me, and talked a little in his way, but all his divinity ran upon confessing my crime, as he called it (though he knew not what

I was in for), making a full discovery, and the like, without which he told me God would never forgive me; and he said so little to the purpose, that I had no manner of consolation from him; and then to observe the poor creature preaching confession and repentance to me in the morning, and find him drunk with brandy and spirits by noon, this had something in it so shocking, that I began to nauseate the man more than his work, and his work too by degrees, for the sake of the man; so that I desired him to trouble me no more." Moll captures well the complicity that surely existed between the Ordinary and the legal system. Defoe, *Moll Flanders*, 285.

THE ALLURE OF IMAGINARY BEINGS

1. Diderot, "Eloge de Richardson," 30.

2. Paul L. Harris, *The Work of the Imagination* (Oxford: Wiley-Blackwell, 2000), 65.

3. On the notion of character as the place of intersection of different codes, see Barthes, *S/Z*. In some manner, Barthes's view coincides with that of a sociologist such as Erving Goffman, who sees social behavior as largely coded. See, for example, Goffman, *The Presentation of Self in Everyday Life* (Edinburgh: Edinburgh University Press, 1959). On the revival of attention to character in literary studies, see Alex Woloch, *The One vs. the Many* (Princeton: Princeton University Press, 2004); Vermeule, *Why Do We Care About Literary Characters?*; Zunshine, *Why We Read Fiction*; Amanda Anderson, Rita Felski, and Toril Moi, *Character: Three Inquiries in Literary Studies* (Chicago: University of Chicago Press, 2019).

4. See also my *Balzac's Lives* (New York: New York Review Books, 2020).

5. Marcel Proust, *À la recherche du temps perdu*, 4 vols. (Paris: Bibliothèque de la Pléiade, 1988), 3:762. English trans. C. K. Scott Moncrieff, Terence Kilmartin, D. J. Enright, and (for vol. 6) Andreas Mayor (New York: Modern Library, 2003), 5:343. I reprise here some of my essay "The Cemetery and the Novel: Persons and Fictions," in *Romanic Review* 111, no. 3 (2020): 357–36.

6. *Recherche* 1:84–85. English trans. *Swann's Way*, Lydia Davis (New York: Viking, 2003), 86–87.

7. See Catherine Gallagher, "The Rise of Fictionality," in *The Novel*, ed. Franco Moretti, 2 vols. (Princeton: Princeton University Press, 2006), 1:351.

8. Pléiade 2:152; ML 2:549–50. I have modified the translation to give a more literal rendering.

9. Jean-Jacques Rousseau, *Julie; ou La nouvelle Héloïse* (1762; Paris: Garnier, 1960), 5. My translation.

10. Pléiade 4:489–90; ML 6:322

11. See Zunshine, *Why We Read Fiction.*

12. See Lynn Hunt, *Inventing Human Rights: A History* (New York: W. W. Norton, 2007)

13. Adam Smith, *The Theory of Moral Sentiments*, ed. D. D. Raphael and A. L. Macfie (Oxford: Oxford University Press, 1984), 9.

14. Pléiade 4:482; ML 6:310

15. See Jacques Rancière, *La Chair et les mots* (Paris: Éditions Galillée, 1989); English trans. Charlotte Mandell, *The Flesh of Words: The Politics of Writing* (Stanford: Stanford University Press, 2004).

16. Freud, "The Ego and the Id," *Standard Edition* 19:29.

17. John Keats, Letter to Richard Woodhouse, October 27, 1818, in *The Letters of John Keats*, ed. Maurice Buxton Forman (3rd ed.; Cambridge: Chadwyck-Healey, 1999). The earlier definition of negative capability comes in a letter to George and Tom Keats of December 1817.

18. Virginia Woolf, *Mr. Bennett and Mrs. Brown* (London: Hogarth, 1924), 4, 18.

19. Henry James, *The Beast in the Jungle*, in *Selected Tales* (London: Penguin, 2001), 437. Other quotations in this discussion: 442.

20. Émile Benveniste, "De la subjectivité dans le langage," in *Problèmes de linguistique générale* (Paris: Gallimard, 1966), 258–66; English trans. Mary Elizabeth Meek, *Problems in General Linguistics* (Miami: University of Miami Press, 1973), 223–30.

21. Conrad, *Heart of Darkness*, 29.

22. Gustave Flaubert, *Madame Bovary* (1857; Paris: Gallimard/Folio, 1972), 253; English trans. Lydia Davis (New York: Viking, 2011). My translation.

WHAT IT DOES

1. See, in particular, Brian Boyd and his desire to create an "evocriticism" in *On the Origin of Stories: Evolution, Cognition, and Fiction* (Cambridge: Harvard University Press, 2010).

2. Friedrich Schiller, *On the Aesthetic Education of Man, in a Series of Letters,* ed. and trans. Elizabeth M. Wilkinson and L. A. Willoughby (1795; Oxford: Clarendon, 1967), 107. In the wake of Schiller there have been other valuable studies of art and play, including Johan Huizinga, *Homo Ludens: A Study of the Play-Element in Culture* (1938; Boston: Beacon, 1955); and Roger Caillois, *Les Jeux et les hommes* (1958; Paris: Gallimard/Folio, 1971); English trans. Meyer Barash, *Man, Play, and Games* (London: Thames and Hudson, 1961).

3. See Thoma Suddendorf and Andrew Whiten, "Great Ape Cognition and the Evolutionary Roots of Human Imagination," in *Imaginative Minds,* Proceedings of the British Academy, ed. Ilona Roth (Oxford: Oxford University Press for the British Academy, 2007), 32–59.

4. Harris, *Work of the Imagination,* 183.

5. D. W. Winnicott, *Playing and Reality* (London: Tavistock, 1971), 14. Other quotations in this discussion: 100, 38 (italicized in original).

6. Sigmund Freud, "Remembering, Repeating, and Working-Through" (1914), *Standard Edition* 12:154.

7. Lionel Trilling, "Freud and Literature," in *The Liberal Imagination: Essays on Literature and Society* (New York: Viking, 1950), 34–57.

8. Sigmund Freud, *Fragment of an Analysis of a Case of Hysteria* ("Dora"), *Standard Edition* 7:15–16.

9. Freud, "Constructions in Analysis," *Standard Edition* 23:257, 23:264.

10. See, for example, Donald Spence, *Narrative Truth and Historical Truth: Meaning and Interpretation in Psychoanalysis* (New York: W. W. Norton, 1984); Stanley A. Leavy, *The Psychoanalytic Dialogue* (New Haven: Yale University Press, 1987); Antonino Ferro, *Psychoanalysis as Therapy and Storytelling,* trans. Philip Slotkin (London: Routledge, 2006).

11. Jerome Bruner, *Making Stories: Law, Literature, Life* (New York: Farrar, Straus and Giroux, 2002), 64.

12. See Strawson, "Fallacy of Our Age," 45. He is quoting from Bruner, "Life as Narrative," *Social Research* 54 (1987): 15, and Sacks, *The Man Who Mistook His Wife for a Hat* (London: Duckworth, 1985), 110.

13. Paul Ricoeur, "Life: A Story in Search of a Narrator," in *A Ricoeur Reader: Reflection and Imagination,* ed. Mario J. Valdés (Toronto: University of Toronto Press, 1991), 435, and Ricoeur, *Temps et récit* (Paris: Éditions du Seuil, 1983), 76, 85. English trans. Kathleen McLaughlin and David Pel-

lauer, *Time and Narrative*, vol. 1 (Chicago: University of Chicago Press, 1990). My translations.

14. Jean-Paul Sartre, *La Nausée* (1938; Paris: Gallimard/Folio, 1974), 63. English trans. Lloyd Alexander, *Nausea* (New York: New Directions, 1959). My translations.

15. On the value of "as if" thinking, see the eloquent attempt to revive Hans Vaihinger and his theory of the "*als ob*" in Kwame Anthony Appiah, *As If: Idealization and Ideals* (Cambridge: Harvard University Press, 2017).

16. I refer to one of the best known of Rudyard Kipling's *Just-So Stories*, first published in 1902.

17. Joseph Carroll, "The Adaptive Function of Literature," in *Evolutionary and Neurocognitive Approaches to Aesthetics, Creativity, and the Arts*, ed. Colin Martindale, Paul Locher, Vladimir M. Petrov (Amityville, NY: Baywood, 2008), 31–45.

18. See Taylor, *Sources of the Self*, 36.

19. Henry James, "The Lesson of Balzac" (1905), in James, *Literary Criticism*, 2 vols. (New York: Library of America, 1984), 2:131–33.

20. See Jean-Paul Sartre, "M. François Mauriac et la liberté," first published in *La Nouvelle Revue Française* in 1939, reprinted in *Situations* (Paris: Gallimard, 1941); English trans. Annette Michelson, "François Mauriac and Freedom," in Jean-Paul Sartre, *Literary and Philosophical Essays* (New York: Collier, 1962).

21. See Sartre, *Les Mots* (Paris: Gallimard, 1964), 122; English trans. Bernard Frechtman, *The Words* (New York: Vintage, 1981), 148.

22. Henry James, "Letter to the Deerfield Summer School," in *Literary Criticism*, 1:93–94.

23. Taylor, *Sources of the Self*, 215.

24. Jean-Jacques Rousseau, "Préface de Julie, ou entretien sur les romans," in *Julie, ou la nouvelle Heloïse*, 739. On stories of the ordinary, see Rachel Bowlby, *Everyday Stories* (Oxford: Oxford University Press, 2016).

25. Wallace Stevens, "Final Soliloquy of the Interior Paramour."

FURTHER THOUGHTS

1. I have made various attempts over the years: see, e.g., "Law as Narrative and as Rhetoric," in *Law's Stories: Narrative and Rhetoric in the Law*, ed.

Peter Brooks and Paul Gewirtz (New Haven: Yale University Press, 1996), and "Clues, Evidence, Detection: Law Stories," *Narrative* 25, no. 1 (2017): 1–27.

2. Arthur Conan Doyle, "The Adventure of the Abbey Grange," in Conan Doyle, *Sherlock Holmes: The Complete Novels and Stories*, 1:1010. I am indebted to the late Robert Ferguson for bringing this story to my attention.

3. People v. Zackowitz, 254 N.Y. 192 (1930). I am grateful to Stephen Schulhofer who, as a visitor to a seminar I was teaching, first made me pay attention to this case.

4. In *Palsgraf*, Cardozo claims that the Long Island Railroad is not responsible for the injuries incurred by Helen Palsgraf because there is too remote a connection between the package of fireworks dropped by a boarding passenger on the tracks and the injuries she suffered. But modern tort law would probably rule differently. And the accident probably did not occur in the manner described by Cardozo, who claims that the explosion "threw down some scales" that injured the plaintiff; it was more likely the stampeding crowd that knocked her down. See John T. Noonan, Jr., "The Passengers of *Palsgraf*," in Noonan, *Persons and Masks of the Law: Cardozo, Holmes, Jefferson, and Wythe as Makers of the Masks* (Berkeley: University of California Press, 1976).

5. Amsterdam and Bruner, *Minding the Law*, 111. Italics in original.

6. Old Chief v. United States, 519 US 172 (1997), 187.

7. Again, see Posner, "Legal Narratology," 737.

8. On this, see Bowlby, *Everyday Stories*.

9. Florida v. Jardines, 569 US 1 (2013).

10. Utah v. Strieff, 579 US ___, 136 S. Ct. 2056 (2016).

11. Michael H. v. Gerald D., 491 US 110 (1989).

12. District of Columbia v. Heller, 554 US 570 (2008). For further discussion of the arguments in *Heller*, see my essay "Law and Humanities: Two Attempts," *Boston University Law Review* 93 (2013): 1437.

13. See, for example, Adam Liptak: "The two sides in the Heller case claimed to rely on the original meaning of the Second Amendment, based on analysis of its text in light of historical materials." "Justices' Ruling on Guns Elicits Rebuke, from the Right," *New York Times*, October 21, 2008;

and Dahlia Lithwick, who comments that *Heller* "revealed the absolute dominance of conservative interpretive theories at the high court... leading more than one commentator to enthuse that regardless of the outcome, after *Heller*, 'we are all originalists now.'" "The Dark Matter of Our Cherished Document," *Slate*, November 17, 2008.

14. Planned Parenthood of Southeastern Pennsylvania v. Casey, 505 US 833 (1992).

15. The Court's logic here evokes Ronald Dworkin's celebrated image of constitutional interpretation as a "chain novel," each new chapter added by a new author who is nonetheless constrained by the plot developed in the preceding chapters. See Dworkin, *Law's Empire* (Cambridge: Harvard University Press, 1986).

16. Gérard Genette, "Vraisemblance et motivation," in *Figures II* (Paris: Éditions du Seuil, 1969), 94; English trans. David Gorman in *Narrative* 9, no. 3 (2001): 252.

17. Barthes, "Introduction à l'analyse structurale des récits," 10; Sontag, *Barthes Reader*, 266.

18. Miranda v. Arizona, 384 US 436 (1966).

19. Stanley Fish makes a similar point in his critique of Ronald Dworkin, "Working on the Chain Gang: Interpretation in Law and Literature," in *Doing What Comes Naturally: Change, Rhetoric, and the Practice of Theory in Literary and Legal Studies* (Durham: Duke University Press, 1989), 94.

20. Ginzburg, "Spie. Radici di un paradigma indiziario," 158–59; "Clues: Roots of an Evidential Paradigm," 96–125.

21. See Erich Auerbach, "Figura," in *Scenes from the Drama of European Literature* (New York: Meridian, 1959), 38.

22. See the similar view argued by Joseph Halpern in regard to *Miranda*: "In contrast to the dissents, the majority opinion employs a comfortable rhetoric that denies and masks change." Halpern, "Judicious Discretion: *Miranda* and Legal Change," *Yale Journal of Criticism* 2, no. 1 (1987): 58. Halpern's perceptive essay as a whole confirms my views of the rhetoric of *Miranda*.

23. Arthur Conan Doyle, "The Red-Headed League," in Conan Doyle, *Sherlock Holmes: The Complete Novels and Stories*, 1: 287.

24. Cooper v. Aaron, 358 US 1 (1958).

25. See United States v. United Mine Workers, 330 US 258 (1947).

26. See Richard Delgado, "Storytelling for Oppositionists and Others: A Plea for Narrative," *Michigan Law Review* 87 (1989): 2411. For effective uses of story that challenge legal assumptions and platitudes, see Patricia J. Williams, *The Alchemy of Race and Rights* (Cambridge: Harvard University Press, 1991).

Index

PETER BROOKS is the author of several books, including the non-fiction volumes *The Melodramatic Imagination*, *Reading for the Plot*, *Psychoanalysis and Storytelling*, *Troubling Confessions*, *Realist Vision*, *Henry James Goes to Paris*, and *Flaubert in the Ruins of Paris*, as well as two novels, *World Elsewhere* and *The Emperor's Body*. He published *Balzac's Lives* with New York Review Books in 2020, and edited two NYRB Classics, Balzac's *The Human Comedy: Selected Stories* and Vivant Denon's *No Tomorrow*. He is Sterling Professor Emeritus of Comparative Literature at Yale.